AF394697

LAND

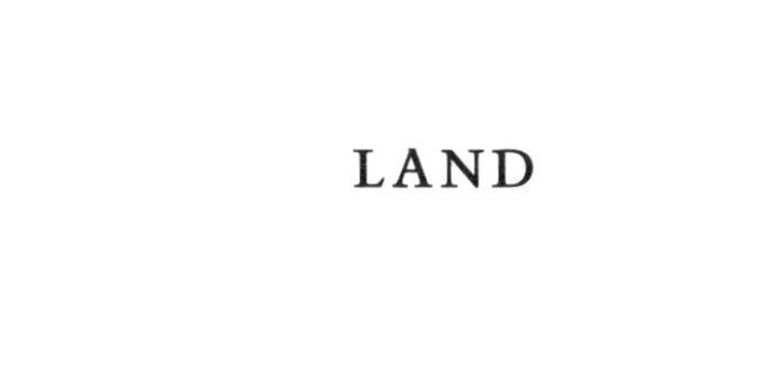

LAND

ANTONY GORMLEY

CLARE RICHARDSON

JEANETTE WINTERSON

The Landmark Trust

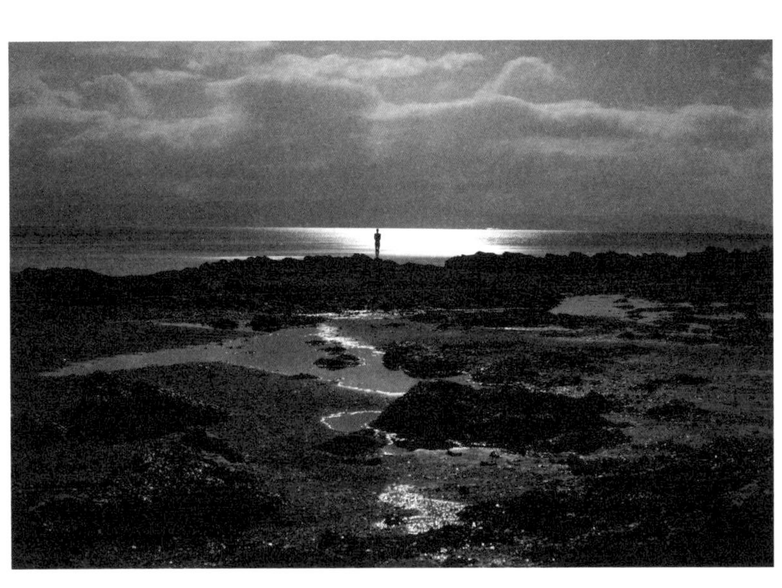

'Although these works are temporary placements…'

A.G.

Temporary. That's how it is for human beings whose time in place is limited. As we walk down the street our footprints disappear; we are already somewhere else.

Temporary is human. We don't live long. Our ancestors lived less long. Graveyards and ruins remind us of the atom and jot of our span.

Against the reality of temporary, humans stage heroic battles for permanence: Archives, museums, endowments, societies for the preservation of… mummies, relics, plaques, even park benches with plaques.

And public monuments. The statue of the fallen hero. The relief of the unsung dead.

Public monuments are semaphore systems made out of solids.

They flag our attention, and they ask us to read their message – not just the plaque on the plinth, but what they stand for. As we pass by them, busy people watching the clock, we register (if we do), some other part of time, where history happened – and in some sense goes on happening. A monument is an X marks the spot, but it is also a story. The story continues because we do.

This tension between temporary and permanent is evident in the way we organise our values and beliefs; monogamy has many purposes – some coercive, some celebratory, but the vow Till Death Us Do Part, is the war-cry of love against time…

Whose final defeat is eternity. The after-life. The unprovable proof that temporary is a category error. We are immortal after all.

Pyramids. Part tomb, part space-ship. The journey to elsewhere. Monuments to magical thinking but also magnetic in their attraction. The human body – house of the human being, so fragile, so temporary, and determined to last forever.

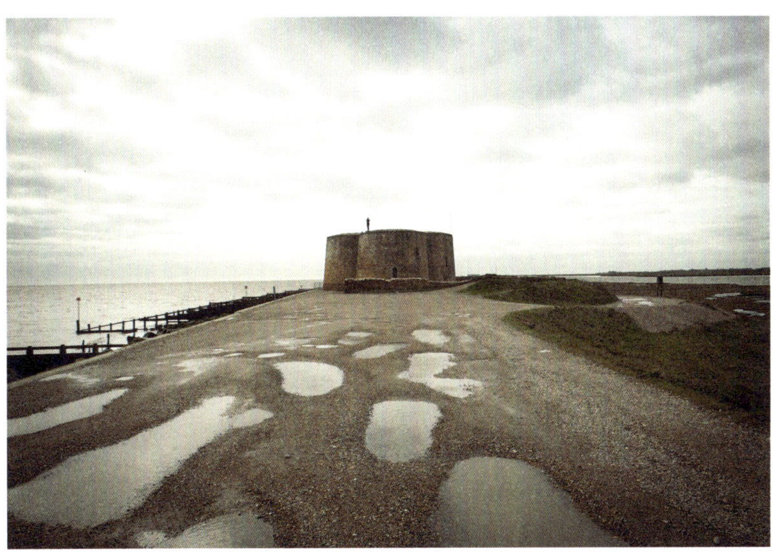

'An opportunity to think and feel the nature of our species…'

A.G.

Antony Gormley works with the human body, encasing its temporariness in more durable material, altering its scale and shape, testing the boundaries of what we recognise and also, what we can relate to. His work isn't representational – he doesn't do the likenesses so familiar from the traditional public statues on their plinths – but it isn't abstract either.

Gormley uses his own body as Everyman, a generic biped that can be stretched or compressed or winged, or as here in the Landmark Trust sculptures, poured into cubes and rhomboids that rust in the weather.

It bothered me, at first, that the five sculptures commissioned to celebrate 50 years of the Landmark Trust would be at their posts for just one year.

But this is only an acceleration of life itself; we are all temporary imprints in a temporary place. Permanence depends on how you experience time. The butterflies I saw sunning themselves on the warm iron body forms will never know that their resting place is gone because the butterflies are gone already.

Anyone can stay in a Landmark, but most will not do so for more than a fortnight. The buildings are permanent, their inhabitants are temporary. So it is right that Antony Gormley's contemplative bodies stay a while but not too long. They slip themselves within the human, natural, and built environments of the Landmarks, suggesting a fourth dimension, which is indeed Time.

The Landmark Trust is interested in the intersection between time and timelessness, which is another way of talking about what is temporary and what is not.

Post-war enthusiasm to rebuild cities and society was heavy-handed with the past; terraced houses were knocked down, tower blocks went up. Farmland became the footprint of new towns, like Milton Keynes, the railways were back-pedalled and road building accelerated. This was exciting but much that was both unique and familiar was being lost.

Each Landmark building commemorates, in its own way, some part of life in the British Isles, life lived differently to ours now. Every visitor arrives in time and experiences timelessness.

This effect is more than a house-style — more than a gentle joke about Old Chelsea crockery, scratchy blankets and lino paint. These buildings aren't time-warps, it's just that time happens differently here.

And that is a relief to those of us who are living in the upgrade generation where temporary had become the new permanent. Why is everything permanently in the process of being replaced? Laptop, smartphone, TV, even your girlfriend. This is the world of zero hours contracts and portfolio careers, short-term rentals and shorting stocks.

What is out there to hold on to?

Antony Gormley bodies, whether in the sea, in the city, or in these remoter landmarks, changed and battered as they are by the elements, contain within their shifting temporality a sense of what is permanent. They are resting places, not only for butterflies and passing birds, but for the eye and the mind's eye.

'A place where a particular human body once stood and anyone could stand…'

A.G.

The bodies are vantage points.

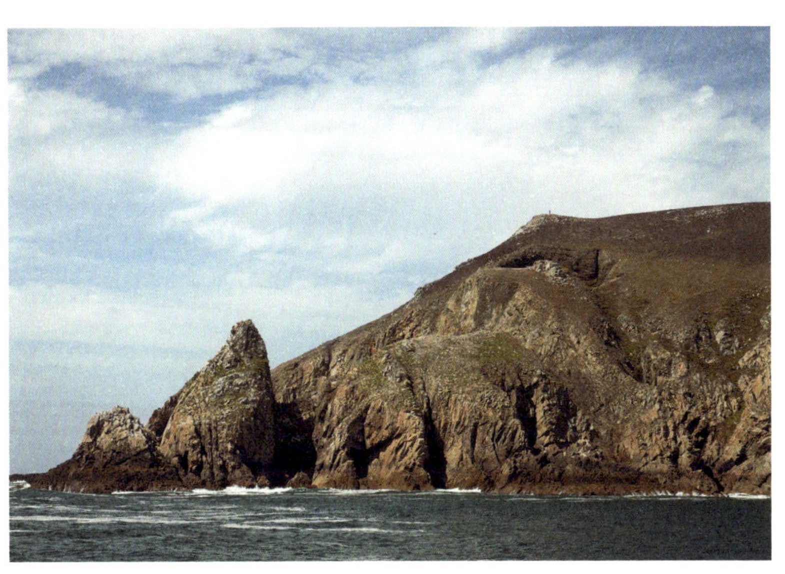

Stand where they stand, look where look, what do you see? Looking is an act of renewal. What have you really looked at today? What did you notice? If you are reading this now, you will be looking at the images of the bodies, and the act of looking will affect you. Art slows us down because we have to stop and spend time with it. We're not glancing from smartphone to screen or skimming the news or checking our train, we're not looking for information or diversion. We're looking. And as we do, the blurriness of rush and dash begins to clear. The world around us stops being signage. We notice the bar of the horizon, the formation of clouds, the reaching branches of trees, the shapes dogs make. The relationship of objects.

The brain relies on data from our senses. Since the beginning of the world we have looked at the world and each other; now we don't. We look at media images and selfies. Kids know their friends best via Instagram.

But, and this is strange but true, art is not a mediated image. Nor is it a representation. Artists see the way dogs scent. This intensity of seeing – the riot of reality in the retina, allows the artwork to release back to us clarity of vision. And we realise that every object, every body, every formation, every grouping, every landscape, every face, is happening both in its own right and in the way that we perceive it. Perception is not simply, *I see the apple*. Perception is *I see the apple* in the way that I see it.

If you do. If you do see it. What did you really see today?

Look. Look at the bodies. Look where the bodies are looking.

And when we see the outside world again, cleansed from distortion and miasma, unmediated, something unexpected happens: we see the inside world too. The inner life of imagination and dream. We are reunited with ourselves.

The picture of the mind revives again.

Standing modestly at their posts, the Gormley bodies are guides. They have something of ancient earth about them — these metal men, as though they have erupted out of the iron core of the world, uncertain of human form, not smoothed by millennia of natural selection, but only now cooled from molten. They could be an older life-form pushed up, tectonically, by a shift in the earth's plates, or returned from a past too old to imagine, through some yawn in time.

They are, with one exception, turned away from the buildings where they find themselves. They are not domestic, these guides, we have to go out and meet them, in clothes fit for a journey.

Where they will take us is up to us.

Saddell Castle, Mull of Kintyre

THE WARRIOR

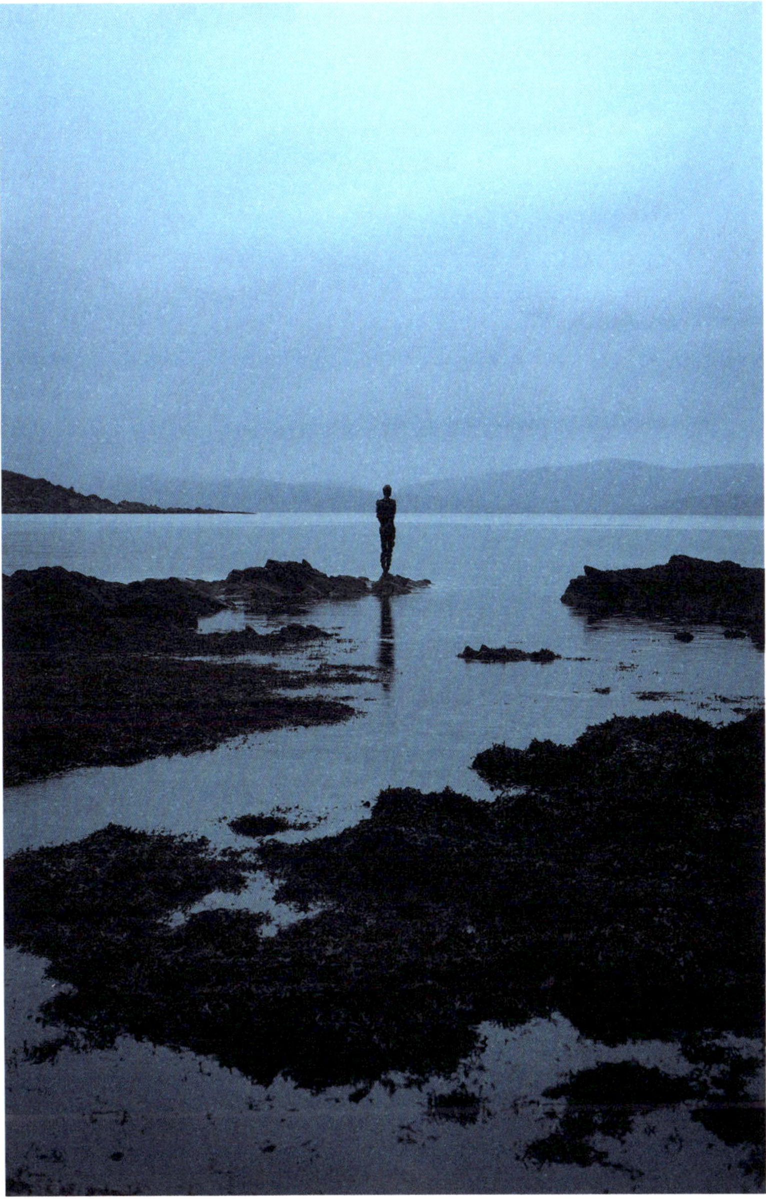

So he seems to me, this body watching the water that at full tide pulls Saddell Castle and Shore Cottage into its reflection.

The castle has a bloody history – a tower house built in the early 1500s from the stones of the ruined Abbey nearby, and not fifty years later, itself burnt and ransacked on the orders of Mary 1st – Bloody Mary, well-named.

By the 1600s, and for 400 years more, the castle belonged to the Campbells who defended their 'fayre pyle' with a battlemented wall-walk and a dungeon from which there was no escape.

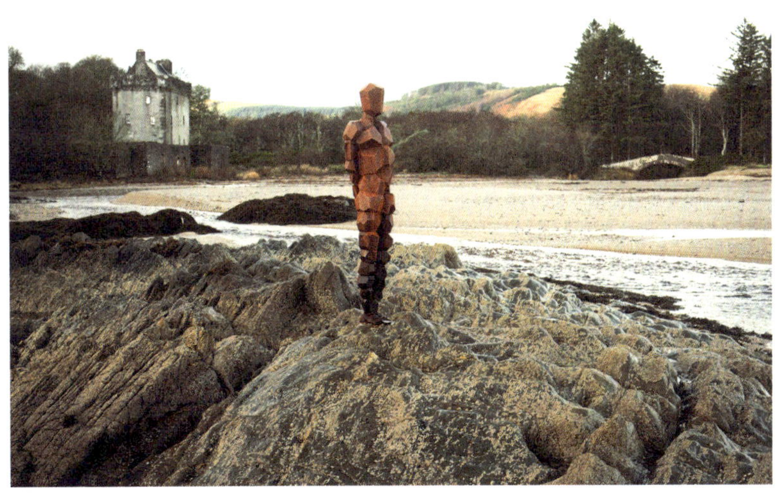

But this is as beautiful and as peaceful a place as you could hope to find on your travels. It sits remote in deep calm, and the sharp rocks wreck no boats now.

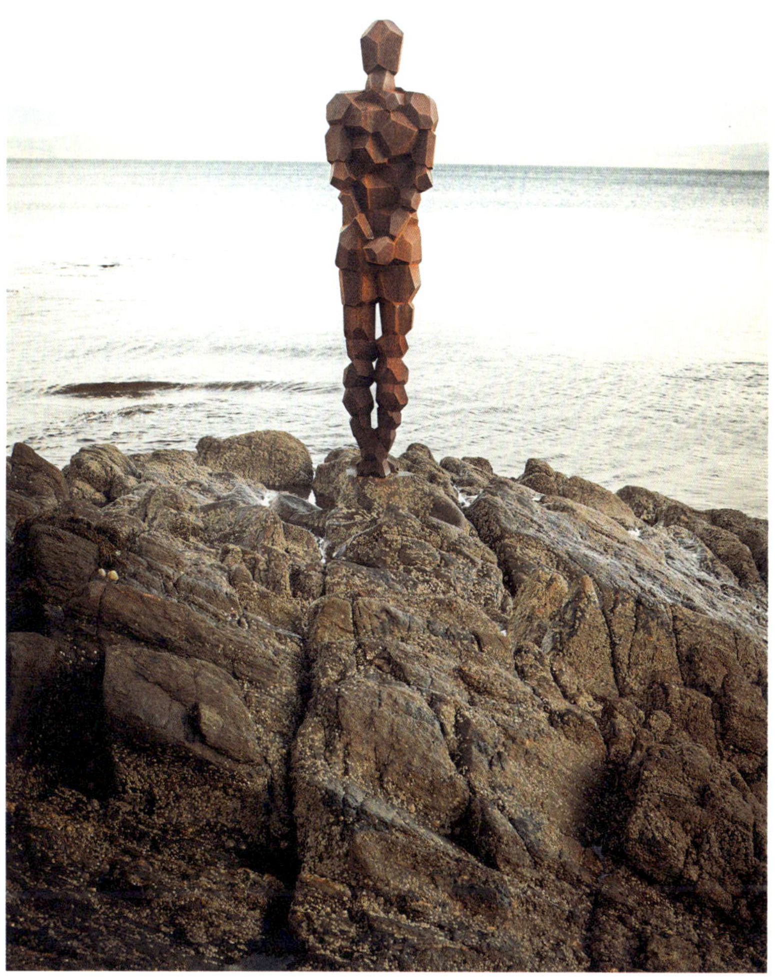

The metal man isn't here to fight any-more. At least to fight no enemies from the outside. He is the true jihadi, the one whose battle is with himself. And that is the final fight – whether you're Luke Skywalker or Harry Potter or Gawain looking for the Grail. Or Moses, who never saw the Promised Land. Or Hamlet, who stands among the murdered and the dead at the end of a play where no ques-tions have been answered – and in a sense where the play begins. The big stories begin alone and end alone.

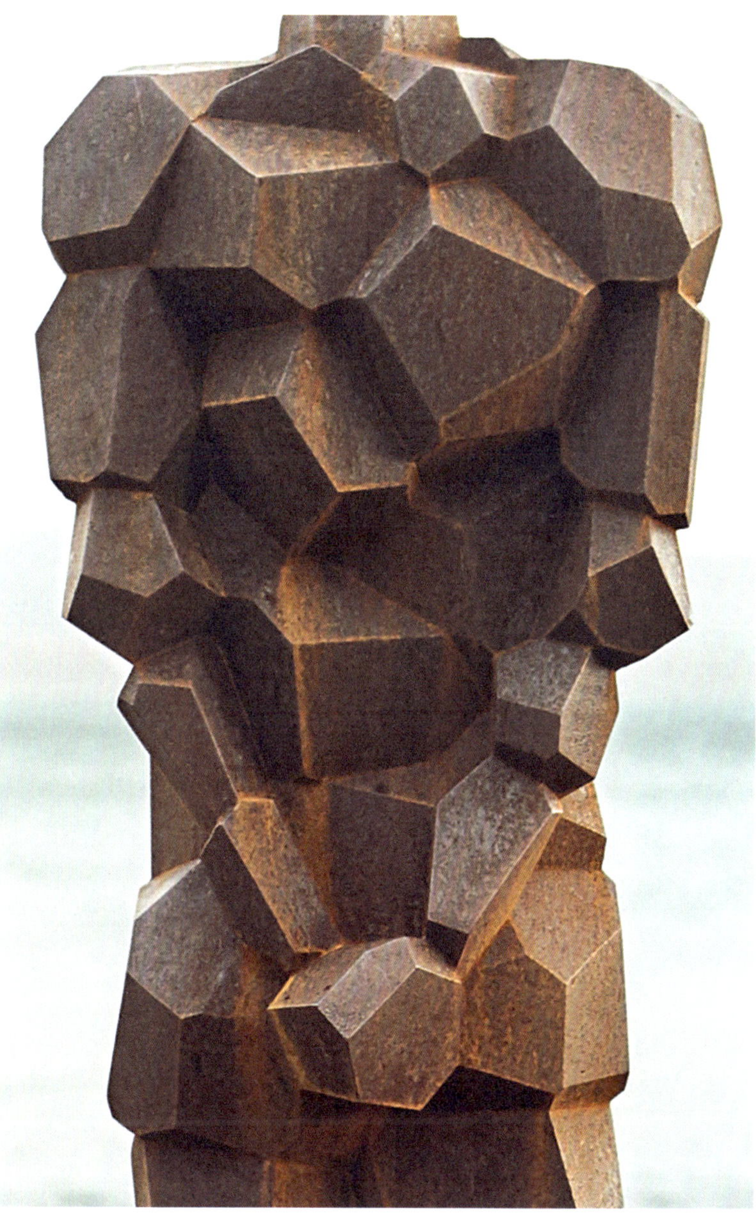

Saddell is a lonely place. The monks who built their Abbey here chose it for its remoteness, and in the ruins of their walls are preserved stone reliefs of crusaders – fighting and voyaging men, used to hardship. The Gormley warrior at the shore is like them. We do not know who he is or what he has seen. We cannot read his thoughts.

But we can read our own.

The iron body is a magnet for thinking.

There are so many stories of statues that suddenly speak or walk. Children endow any inanimate body, human or animal, with magical properties of sympathy and power.

36

This metal man, both near to and far from our own human forms, waits like a warrior-confessor. What is it that you have seen? What is it that you want to say? And I think it would be something to reach the same point of stillness, the end of action and the beginning of contemplation.

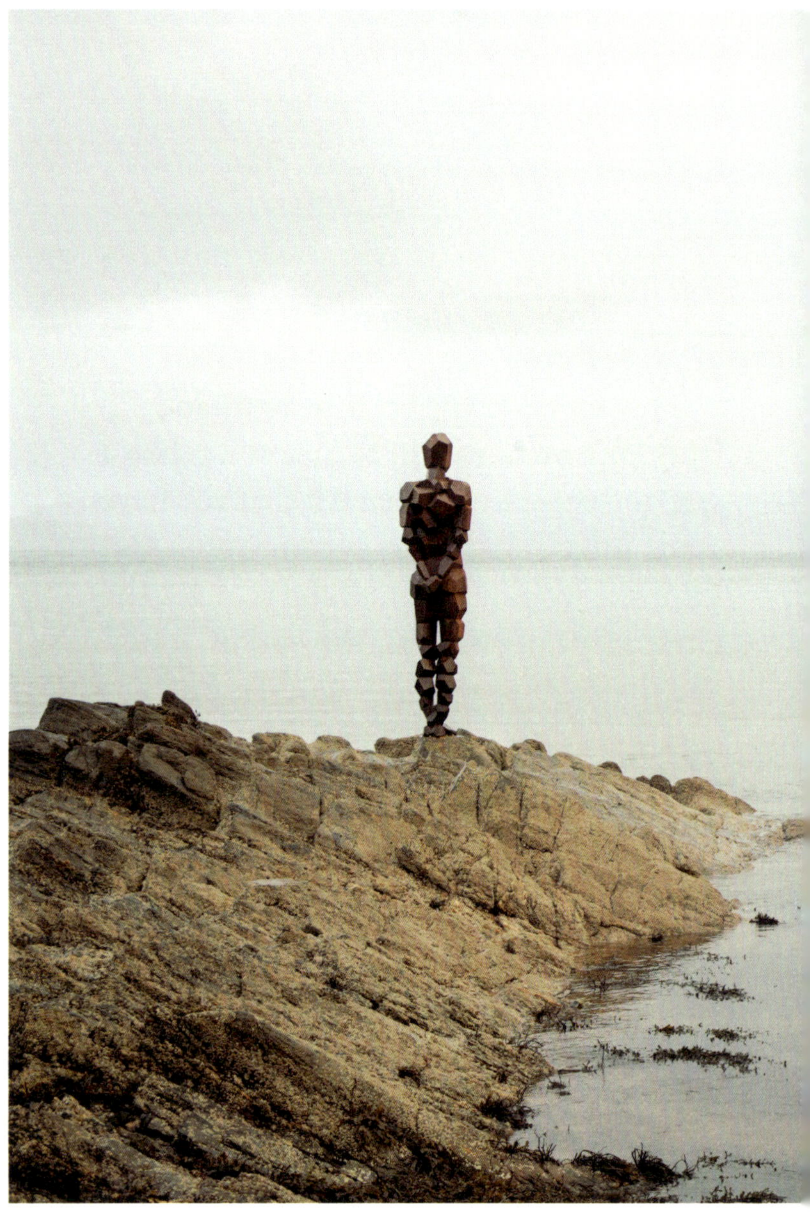

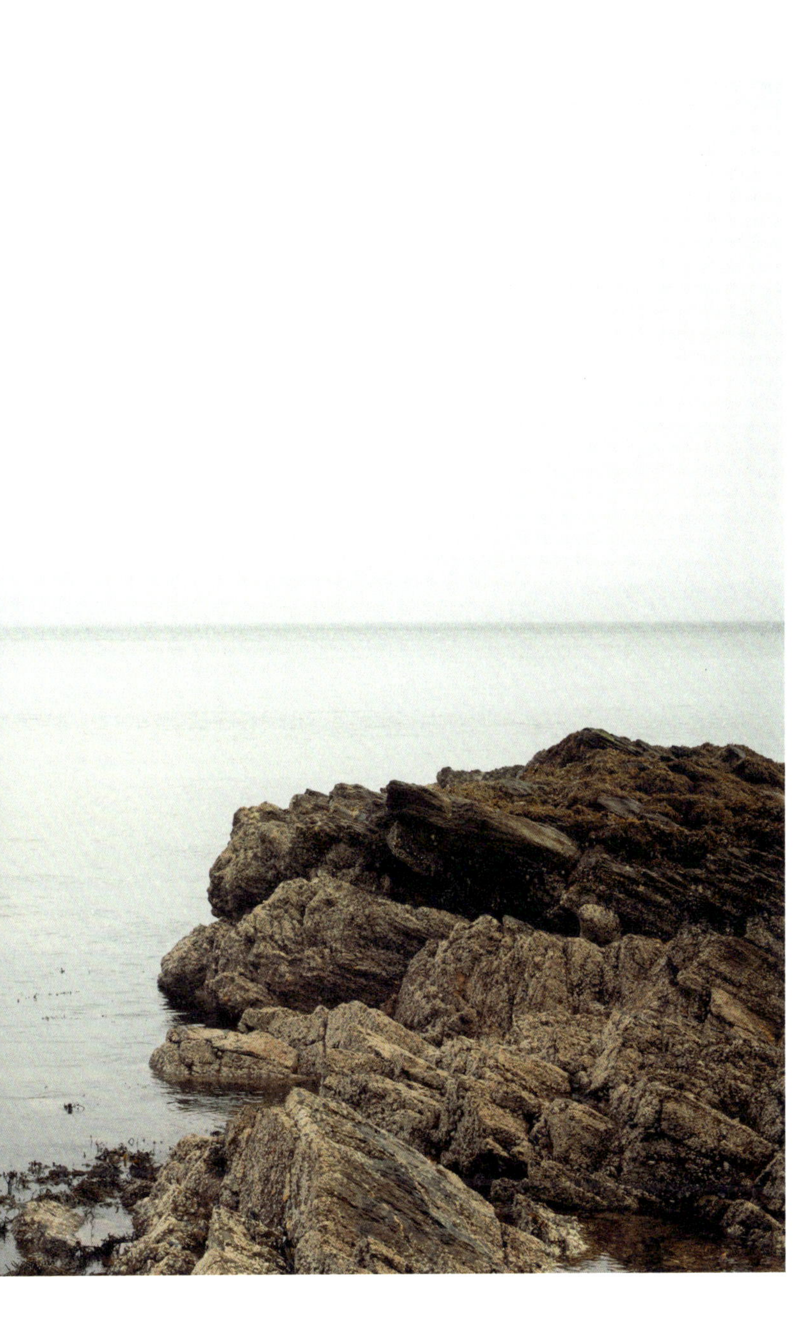

Outside of the knowing gaze of the gallery or the self-consciousness of the exhibition space, outdoor sculpture must take its chance with the rough and ready of everyday life, and with the elements and the weather. It becomes a local object, not folded into the landscape, but unfolding the landscape, because it catches our eye, in the way that movement does – even though it is in itself unmoving.

At Saddell, the tide rises and falls round his body. The seals came to look at him, their whiskered dog-heads bobbing up beyond the rocks.

The Landmark housekeeper said to me, 'I didn't think much of him when he first came – I thought, what's the point of that?' Then she says, a little embarrassed, 'But now I say good morning to him when I get here'.

She looks at him, where he stands undefeated by time. 'I'll miss him', she says.

Martello Tower, Aldeburgh

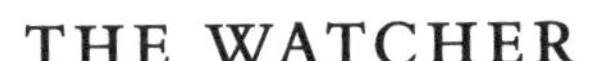

THE WATCHER

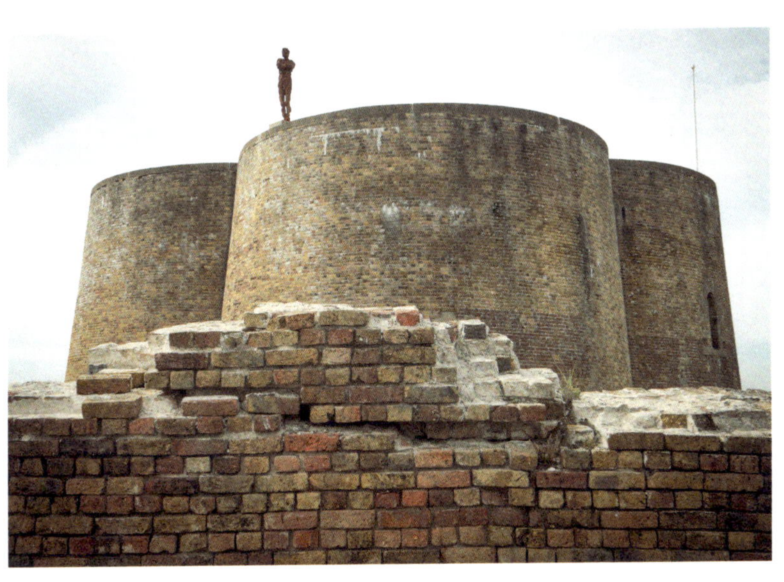

Martello Towers – what's left of them – stand on the east coast of England, part history, part madness.

Begun in 1803 as a response to the bellicose bawling of Napoleon across the Channel, their purpose was to house garrison and gun batteries on the stretch of coast most likely to be invaded.

In spite of the victory of the Battle of Trafalgar in 1805, and the routing of the French navy, Martellos went on being built.

Aldeburgh was the biggest, a million bricks-worth, with pumped-up shoulders to take extra guns. It was completed in 1812 – but by 1815 Napoleon had been decisively defeated at Waterloo.

The body here on look-out from the top of the tower stands like a gun salute to the sky.

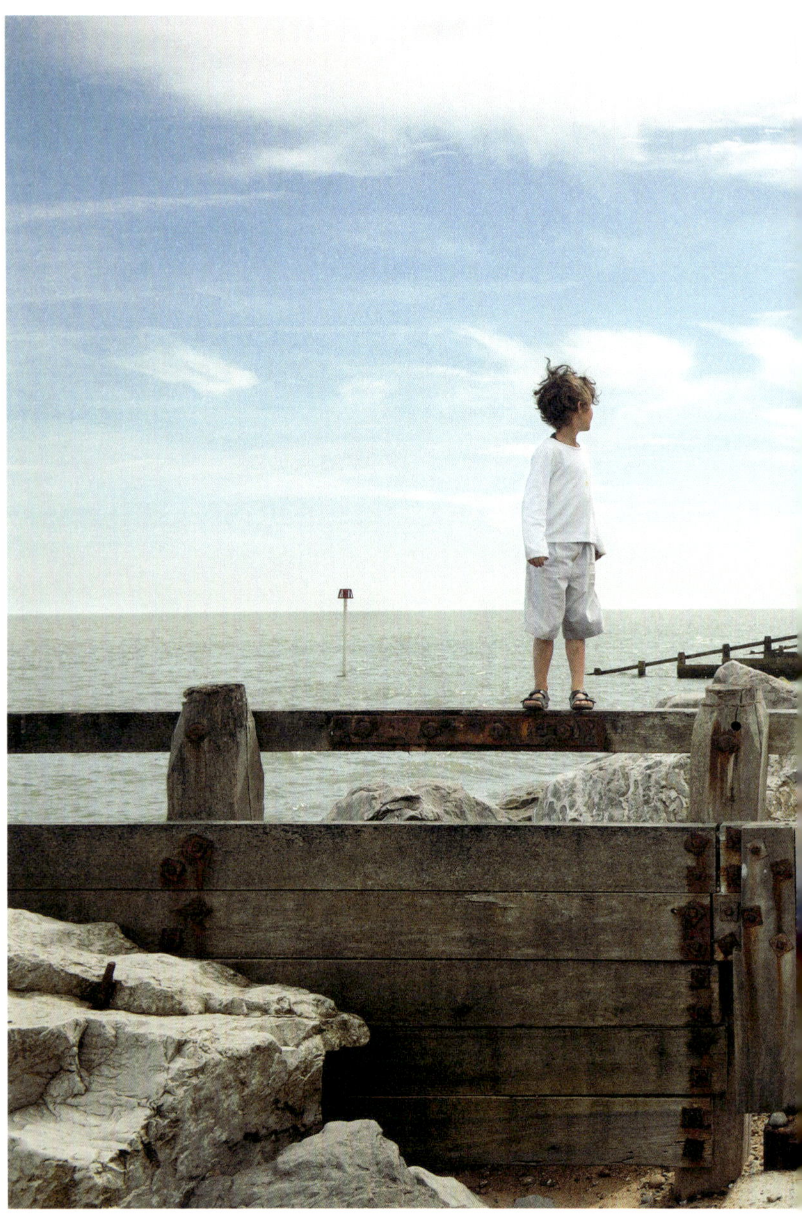

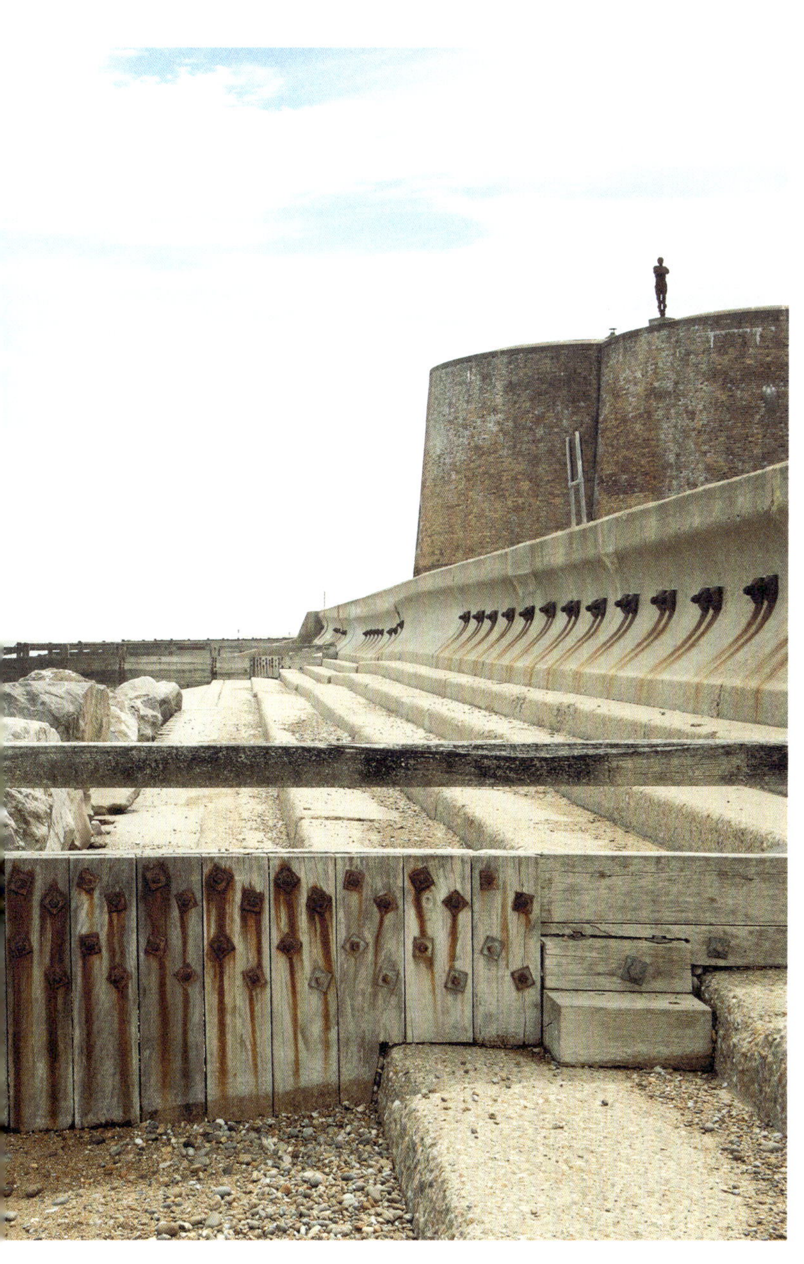

Skies here are high, like sopranos are singing them. Clouds as big as the Martello crowd in a rig above it. The massy shoulders of the tower dominate the shingle. There is an exhilarating feeling of scale and height – an illusion of light and vast open space I think – because the Martello is not more than 40 feet high. But in this bigness, is the small defiant body of a man who might be conducting an orchestra of clouds.

The glory of public art is that it's there for us to look at. The tragedy of public art is that we don't look at it.

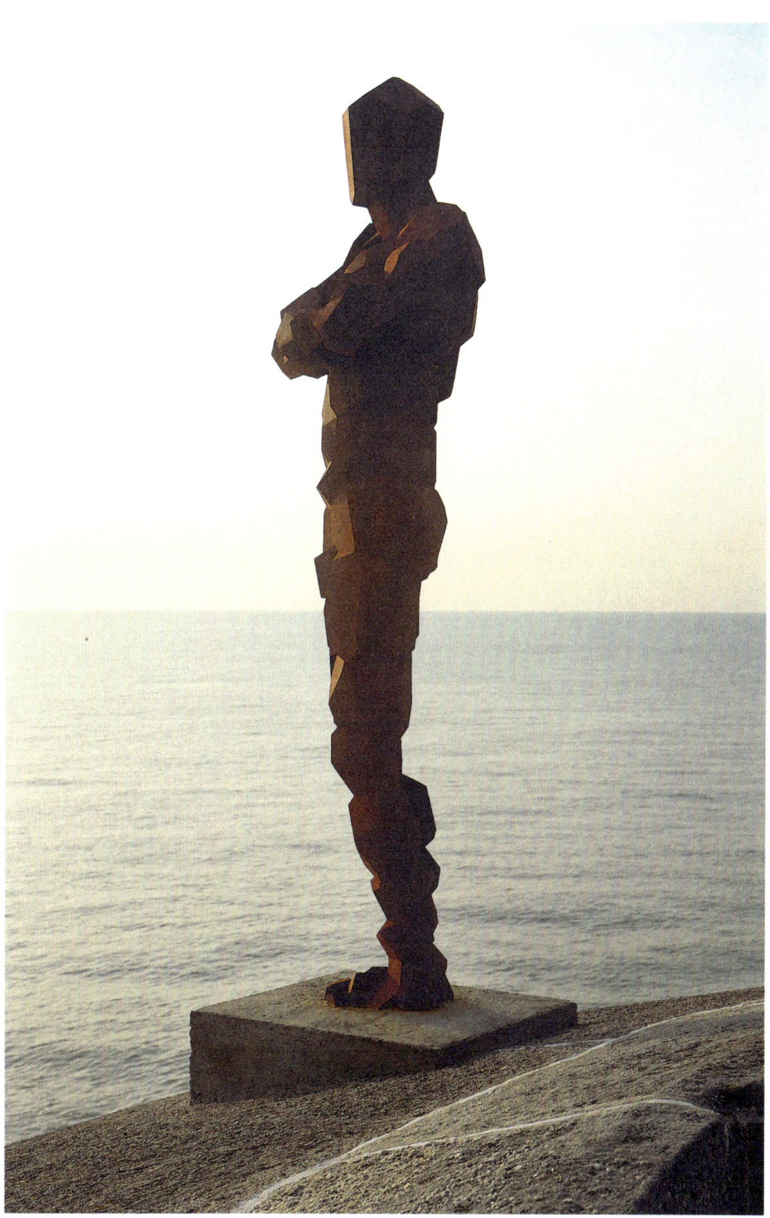

Admiral Nelson, responsible for curbing Napoleon's ambitions at Trafalgar, has his statue, plinth, plus lions, in London's Trafalgar Square. Tourists admire them. Londoners walk on by. The fourth plinth in that square is an initiative to coax the daily thousands passing through and round the square to actually look at what is there. Antony Gormley's project, *One and Other*, proposed that a rotation of ordinary people should stand on the plinth – the human body as its own sculpture and artwork.

Thus positioned, the distance between viewer and viewed disappears. Thus positioned, the passer-by becomes the object of his own attention (and the attention of others who would also pass by).

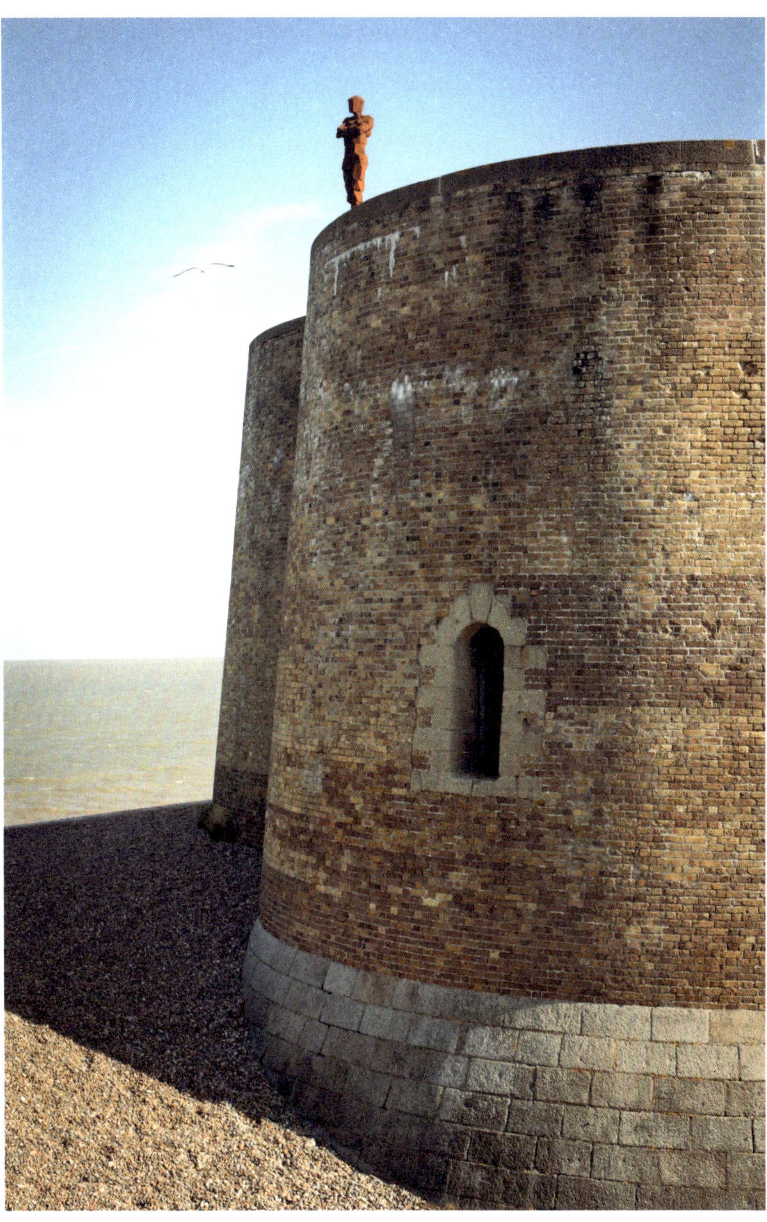

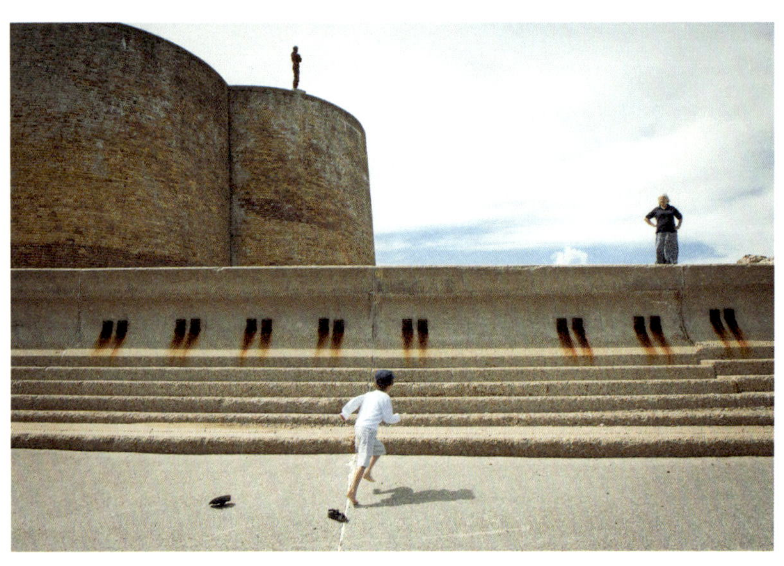

54

Some of the genius of Gormley's bodies is in their placing. He knows where to site them so that they make significant formal impact – in harmony with or counterpoint to their setting – but also so that they will draw the eye and hold it there.

The body, complete in its own right, then becomes the focus of a larger composition, where all elements around the body take their place in the visual experience.

At Martello, this is dramatic – like a moving tableau – because the sea and sky change all the time – they are the permanent temporary.

And so anyone walking along the shingle, or at sea in a small boat, can for a while appreciate themselves as part of a work of art. The observer and what is observed are not separate after all.

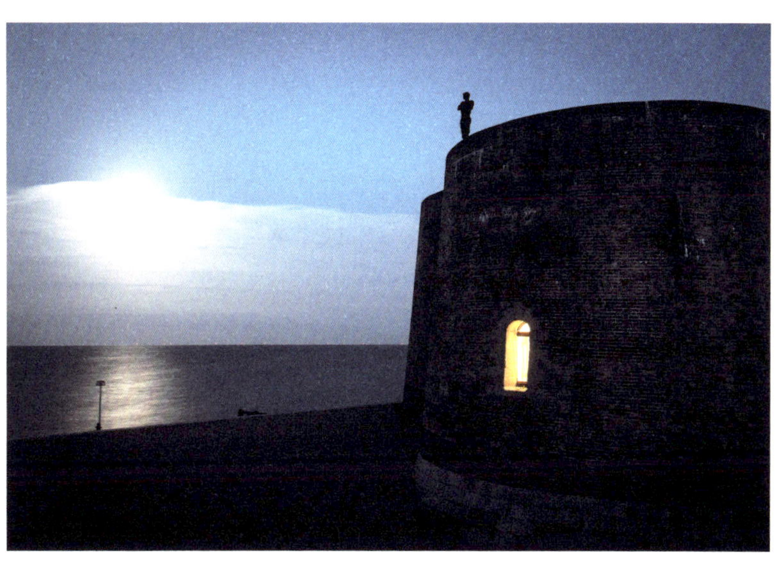

Clavell Tower, Kimmeridge Bay

THE WOUNDED MAN

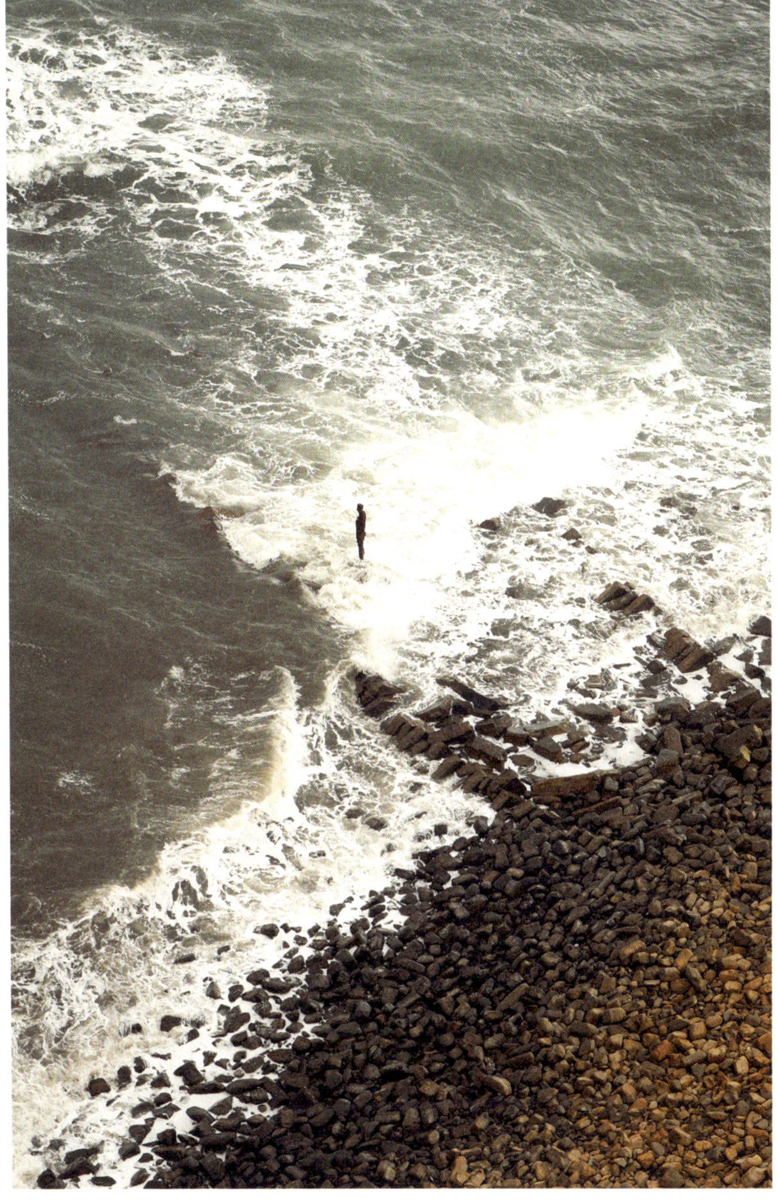

This body was the temporary of the temporary. Twice skittled by boulders, lifted easily on the fierce waves, he was taken away in winter like a wounded king.

When I saw the body standing in the water beneath the tower I thought of Kurwenal, guarding his fatally wounded master Tristan, and waiting for the sign of a sail; the sign of Isolde coming at last to where Tristan will die in her arms.

The wounded hero is a persistent icon. He's older than Christ – Ulysses returning to Ithaca is recognisable by the long wound on his thigh. Achilles, literally, has his heel. King Arthur, stabbed by Mordred, is returned to some mysterious infinity by the Lady of the Lake. The Fisher King lies bleeding. Gulliver has a knee injury. Harry Potter bears his scar.

People talk about art as consolation or catharsis or challenge or confrontation, or sometimes just chaos and confusion.

But art is for the wounded. And that's why it's for us all.

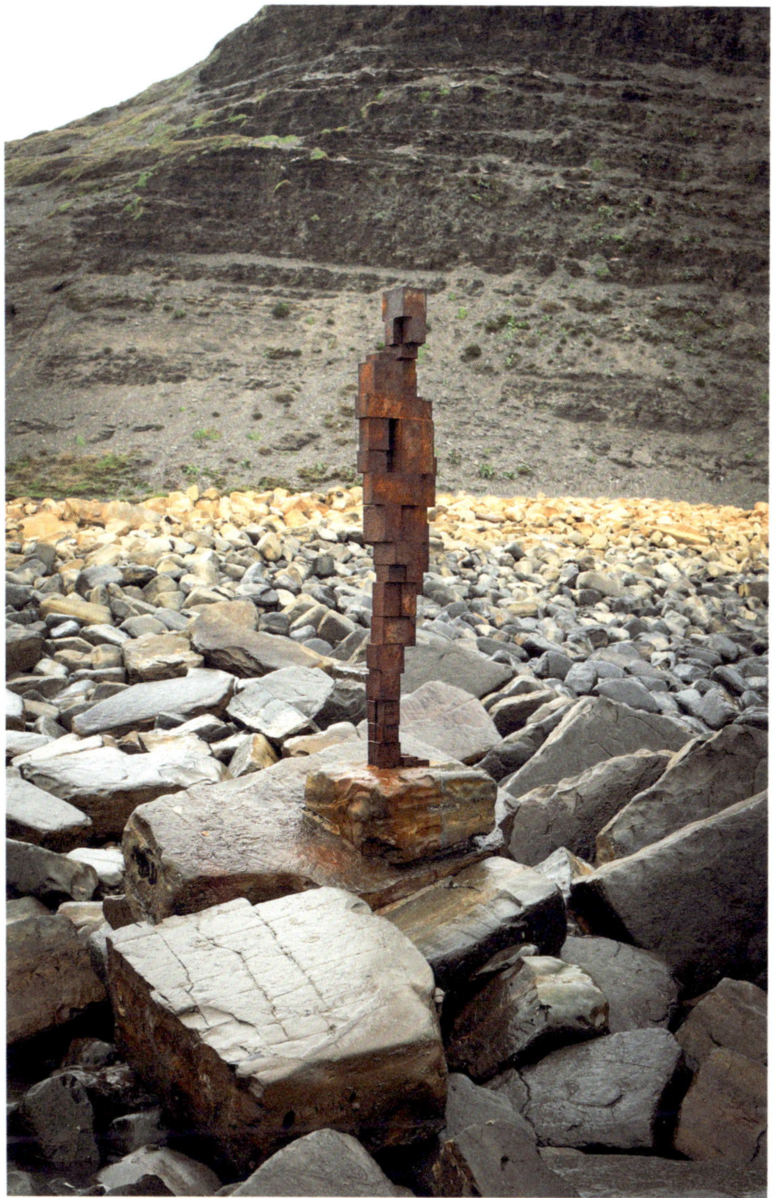

The Gormley bodies, with their rough exposed muscles and weathered bodies, their blocked-out faces, their extreme surfaces, are like medieval pietàs; not Mary holding the dead Christ: Everyman holding us. Not in their arms – on their backs. There's strength here. There's waiting here. Patience. A pietà is a place to leave your burdens.

And if you scramble down into the water. And if you transfer all the tension in your body. And if you sit up high on the cliff and aim your mind at him.

Art objects are there to carry what we can't bear.

Why has this been forgotten?

66

There is great humanity in the Gormley bodies, placed here or elsewhere. Their human shape makes them approachable. Their abstraction gives them the power of a shrine.

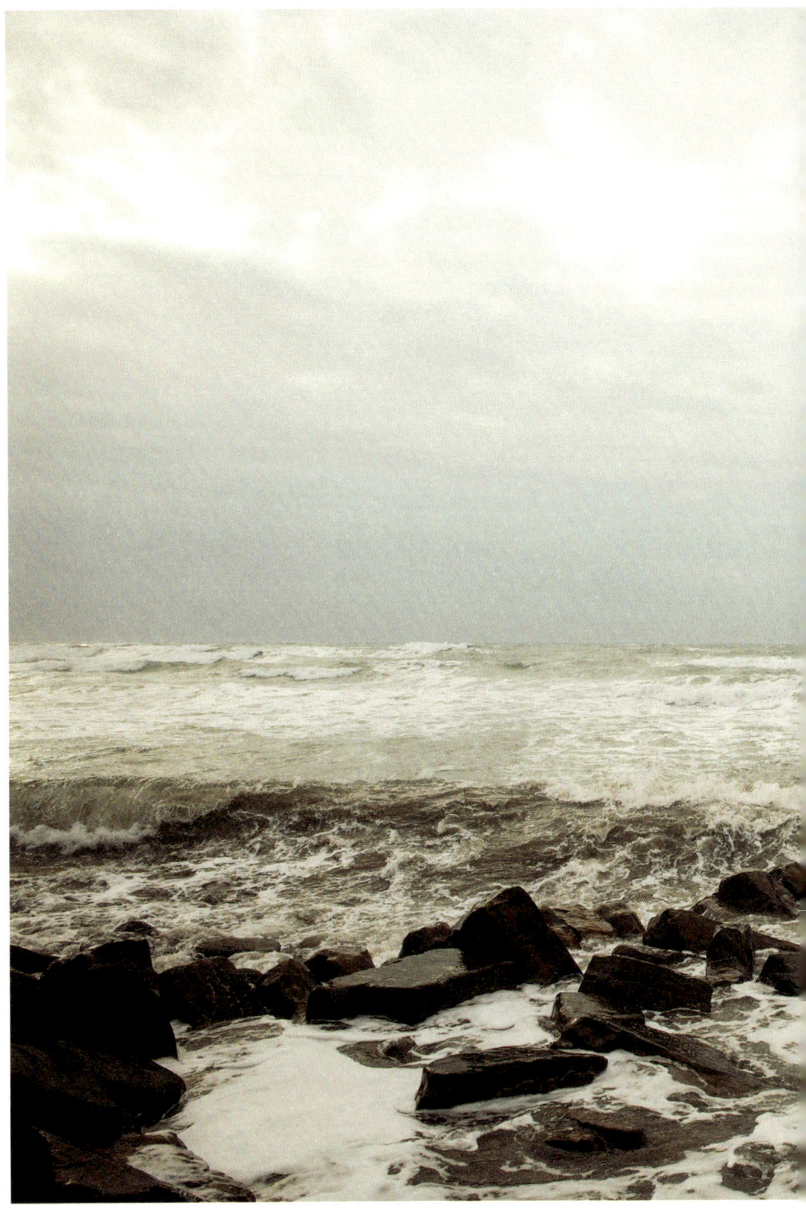

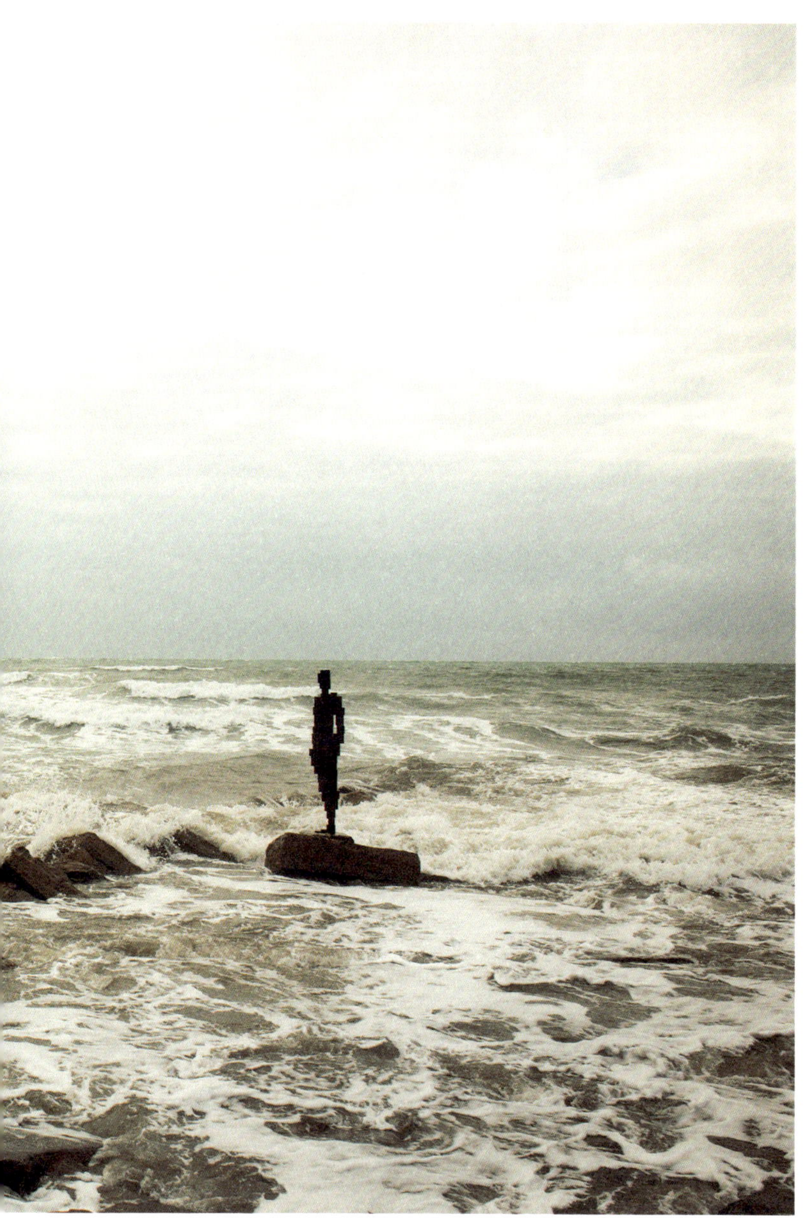

One of the jobs of religion was to manage pain. Religion can't do that for most of us now. I don't think art is a substitute for religion – I think religion and art lie on the same frequency – which is why they have been such a powerful partnership across time.

What is that frequency?

An attunement to the fact that life has an inside as well as an outside. We are accountable to it, and must account for it – the reality not measured empirically, scientifically, materially, or by any other measure that reads no meaning deeper than self- interest, success, or selfish genes.

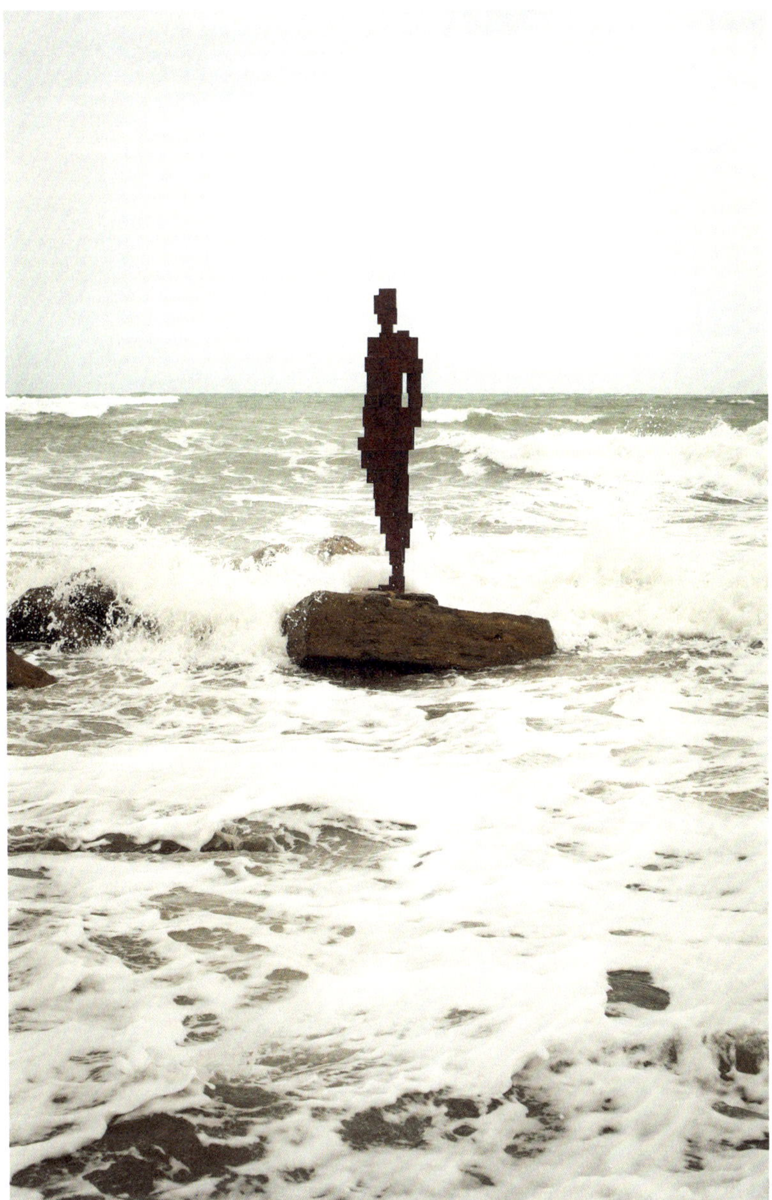

A body standing in the sea cannot
answer to this. But the body standing in
the sea honours the question. Who am I?
What am I?

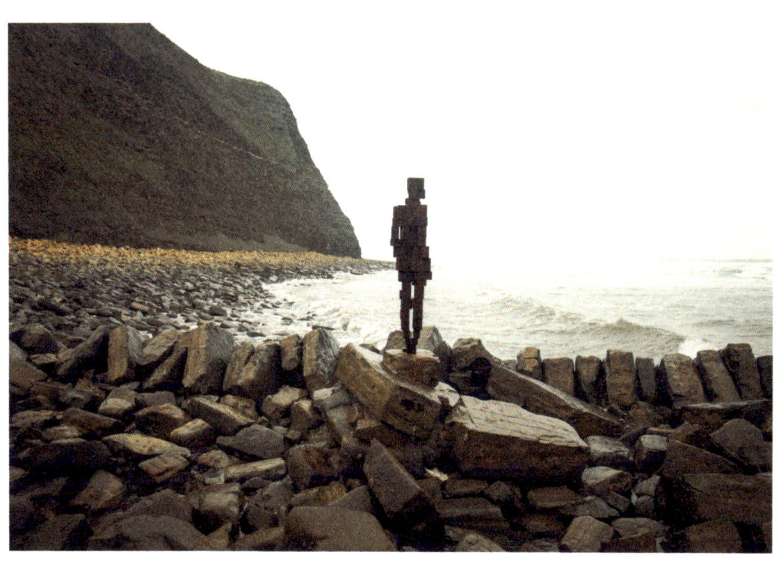

Antony Gormley returns to the same form — the human form — to create a questioning space. Questions are more reassuring than answers. Answers, even good ones, right ones, are temporary. The questions return — each generation must ask them and try to answer them again. It's the clichés that cause the trouble.

Suffering is inevitable. Some wounds will never heal. I don't imagine the Gormley bodies are like totems with healing powers, but I know that the solid presence of the art object is strong enough to carry pain.

Art for art's sake? I never believed that. Art for our sake?

Yes.

Lengthsman's Cottage, Lowsonford

THE WANDERER

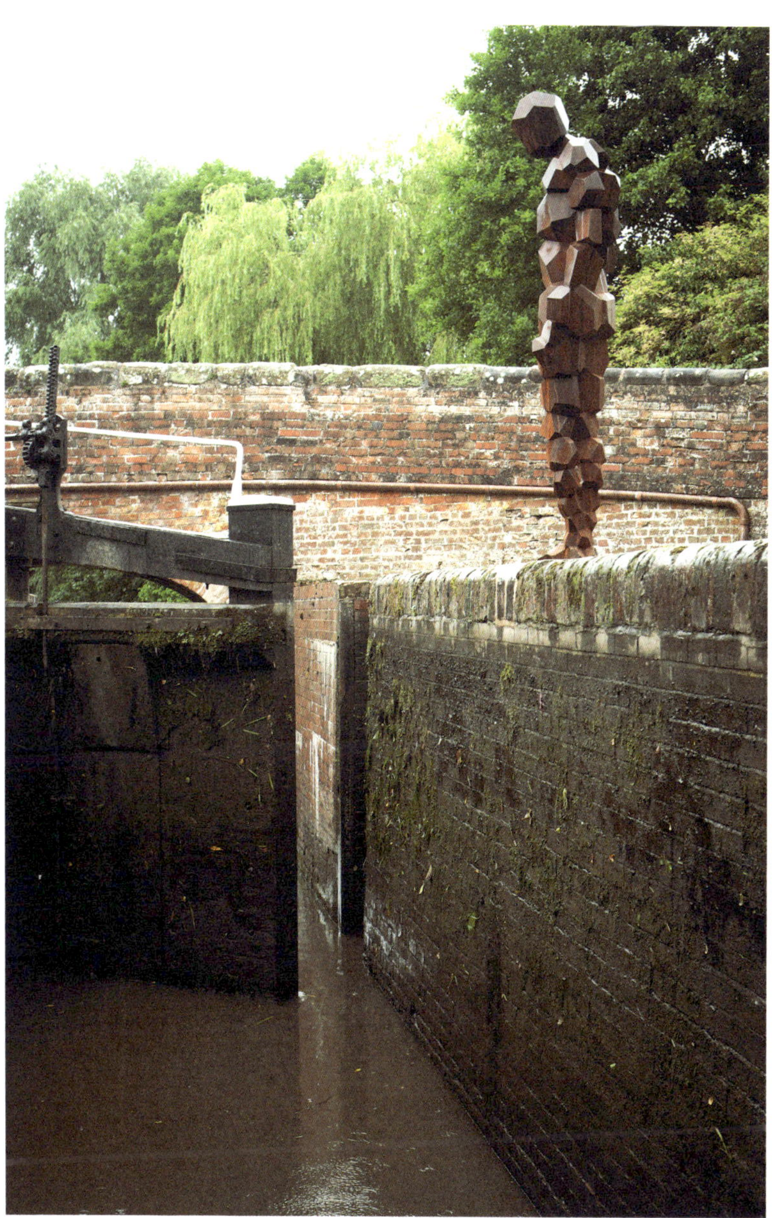

The lightest and loveliest of the bodies. The relax in the metal is impressive. How do you make iron look laid-back?

And the pleasure of touching. We're so used to art being Do Not Touch. Ropes. Lighting. Security. The Gormley men are the best of public art – you can put your arms round them.

Antony Gormley's decision to site one body on this inland waterway acts as a commentary on the rest. The wild beauty of Saddell and Lundy, the shingle stretching into sea and sky at Aldeburgh, and the dramatic surge of the coast at Clavell Tower, are here subsided into the South Stratford Canal.

This is the only site where the water is contained. The body looking down might have walked here. He might be a relative of the Tin Man in Oz. He has humour, time to spare, he is friendly to children and dogs.

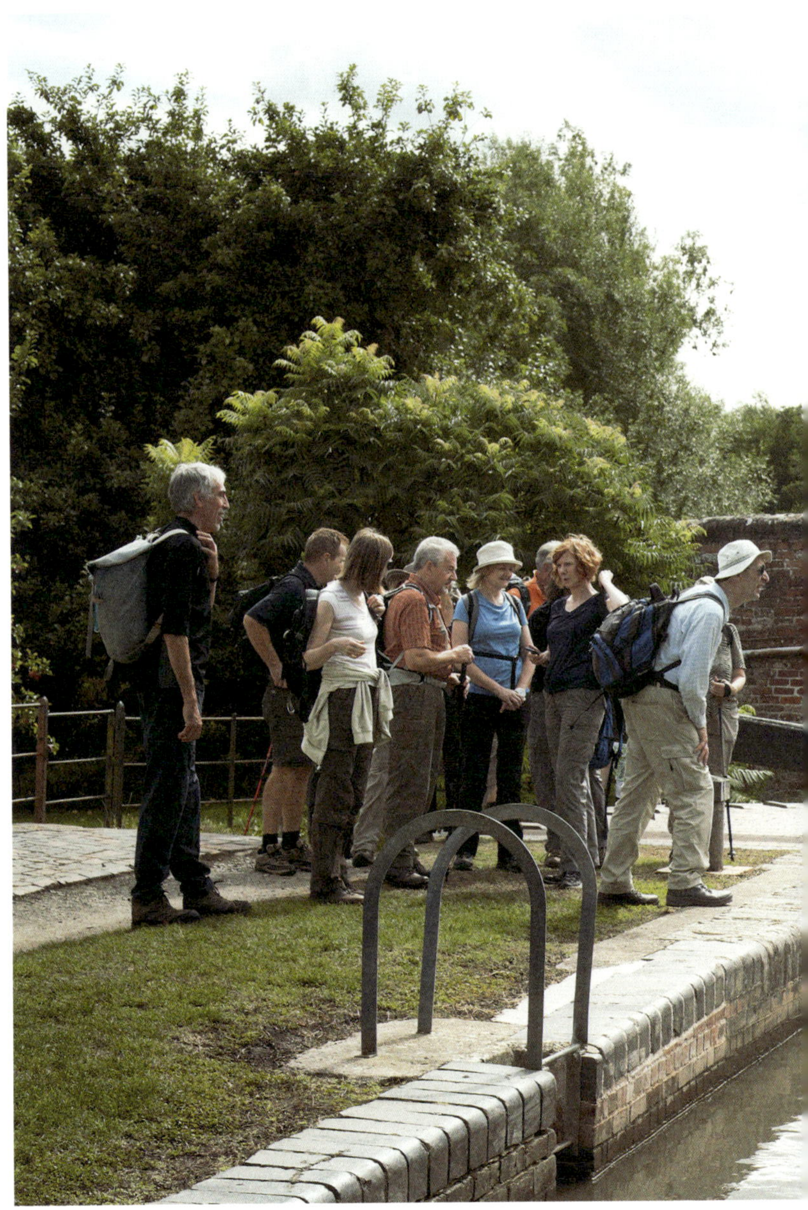

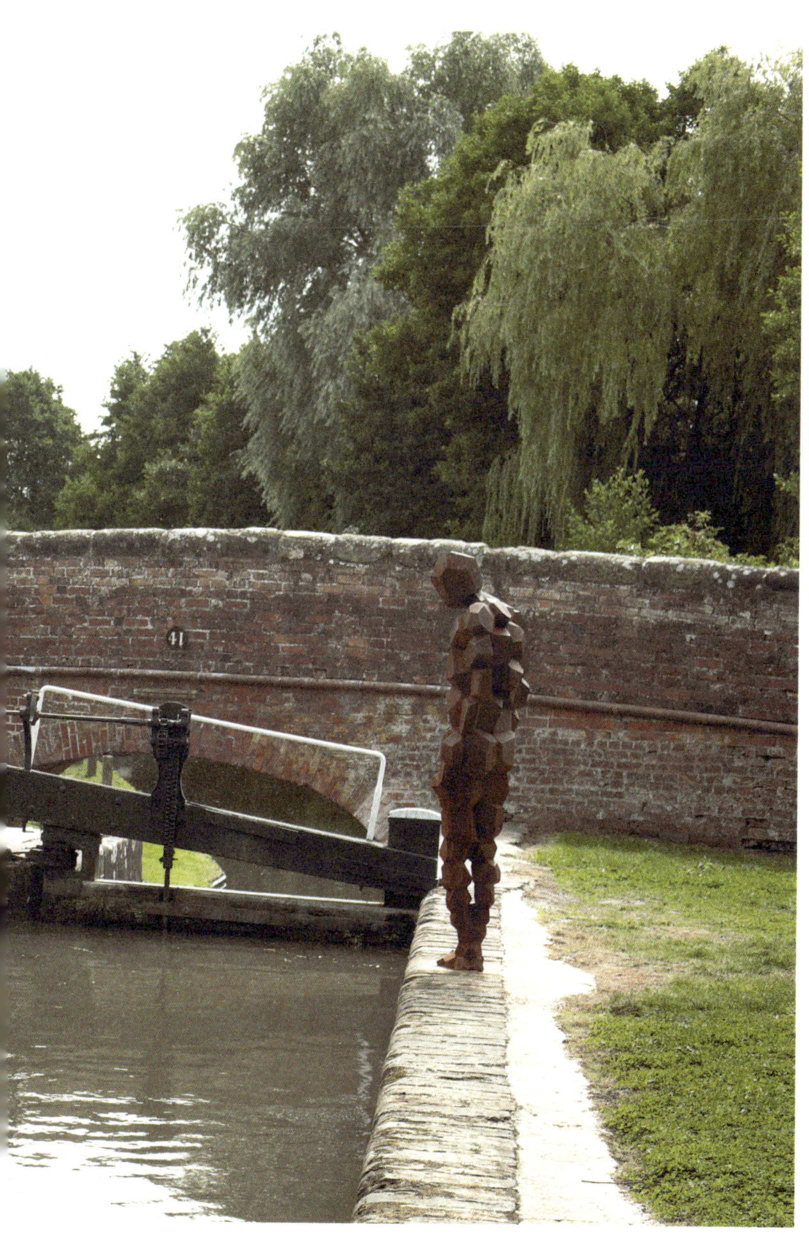

There is a long tradition in English life and narrative of the Tramp. A product of the early industrial revolution – like the canals – the Tramp was sometimes a Journeyman looking for work, sometimes a small-holder dispossessed from the land or hoping for a better living among the rapid growth of the factories. Sometimes the Tramp was a religious non-conformist. Sometimes he was a poet. Wordsworth and Coleridge were both great walkers – covering vast distances of England, and writing their poems as they went.

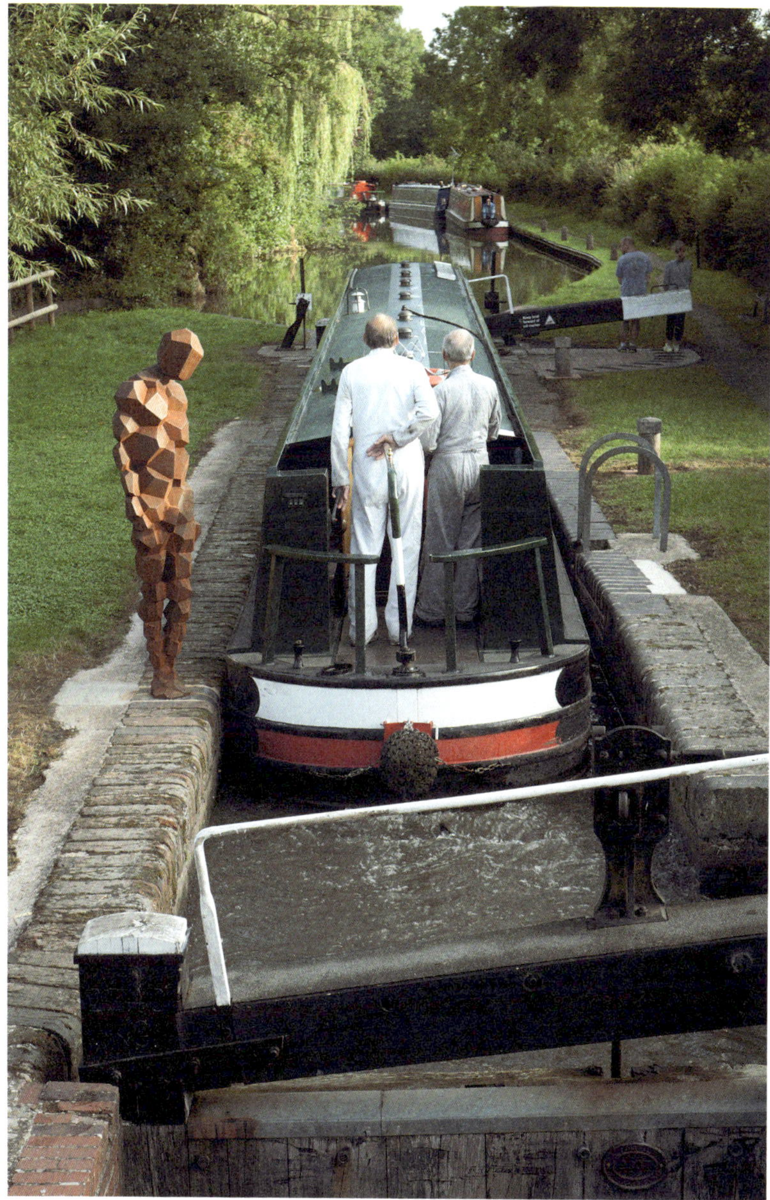

Canal traffic went at walking speed. The speed of our bodies is a deeply personal rhythm. Slow? Fast? And it's a rhythm we're much less accustomed to than those who went before us. We still *go* walking, but with cars and mass transit, few of us walk.

This body is a memory-point for the life we no longer live.

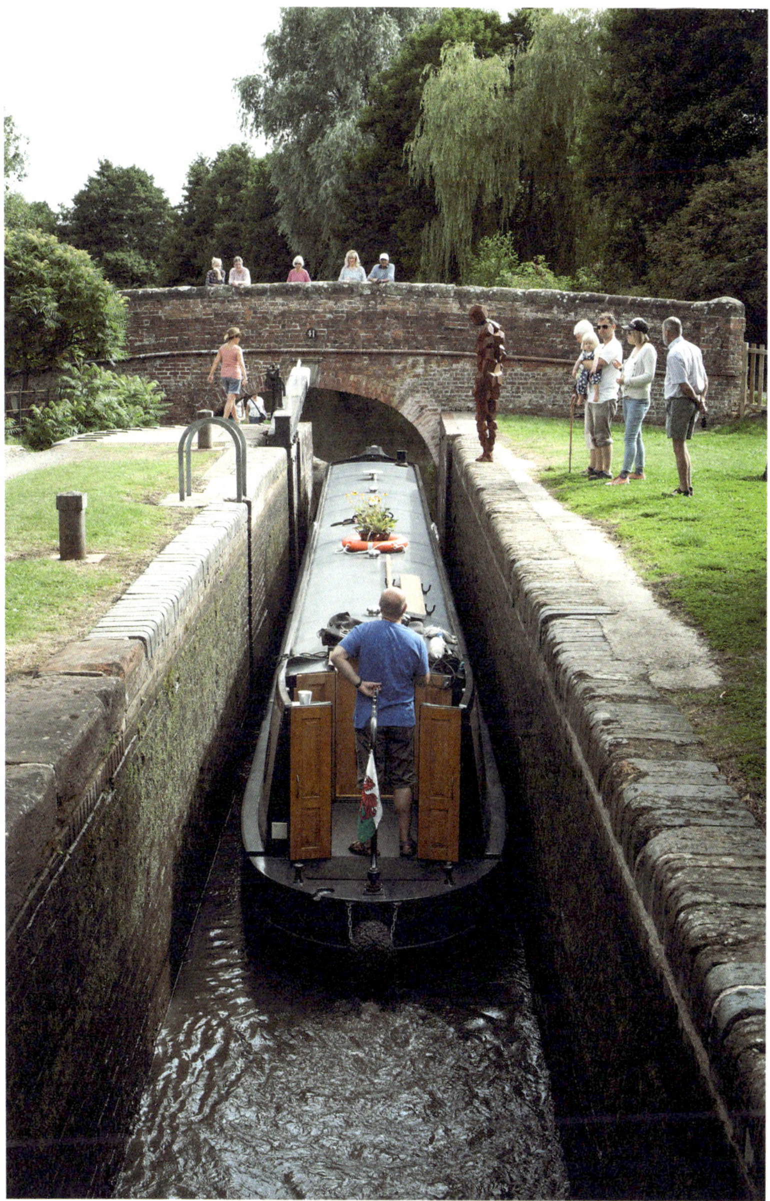

The canal stretch at Lowsonford is spasmodically busy as knots of tourists come and go, but the chug of the canal boats rising and falling in the lock is the true speed of the place. There is time to stop and stare. Time to waste. Time to daydream. The Landmarks all play tricks with time, but this one is proof that time is what we make it.

Only the coming of the railways – the canal system's demise – standardised time. Why? Railways need timetables and timetables need fixed time. Local time was haphazard, approximate, moveable. Sunsets and sunrises are different in different parts of the country.

From 1840 onwards, time moved towards what it is now – a commodity. GMT was adopted as late as 1880. Until then, time kept trying to move at its own pace – that is, the pace of the natural, pre-industrial world. Can you tell a cow it must calf in exactly one hour?

Humans find time stressful now – mainly because we cannot find time at all. We have lost, not leisure exactly, but a sense that there is time enough to do what needs doing and some left over to enjoy. We thought we could become Time Lords; instead we live in a clockocracy.

Art objects object to standardised time. There is no such thing as standard time in the making of a piece of work. It takes as long as it takes. And creativity has a way of stretching and compressing time all at the same time. Then there is the curious truth that art lives in the present – we can see the date of the object, but it doesn't live in the past, the way a suit of armour does, it lives now; that is why we're still affected by those paintings, books, plays, sculptures, the piece of music. And because the art of the past lives in the present, we are all time travellers in its company.

We are connected across time, not atomised on our little raft of Now.

Time, the way we live it, is strict and unforgiving, but it is also temporary time, provisional, makeshift, just for now.

Real time, or significant time, is permanent, by which I mean it doesn't pass. Action happens in time, meaning doesn't. 'We had the experience but missed the meaning' is how T. S. Eliot put it, because the experience passes, but the meaning holds. We are only in thrall to time if time is momentum without meaning.

Wandering is not purposeful. It isn't the planned route or the charity walk. A lot of art is made while wandering about, either in your mind or on foot. It's a necessary aimlessness. It's the antithesis of goal-orientated, set your sights how-to manuals and inspirational talks. It isn't organised.

The body here, pausing for a while opposite the lock-keeper's cottage, is a moment in time that is not measured.

Those moments that seem to last forever, and those moments where time collapses. The way we remember is not chronological. One memory leads to others, not sequential – often separated by years, but in our minds there is no distance.

The body is a memory-point.

South West Point, Lundy

THE WOMAN

Lady, whose shrine stands on the promontory,
Pray for all those who are in ships…

T.S. Eliot, *Four Quartets*

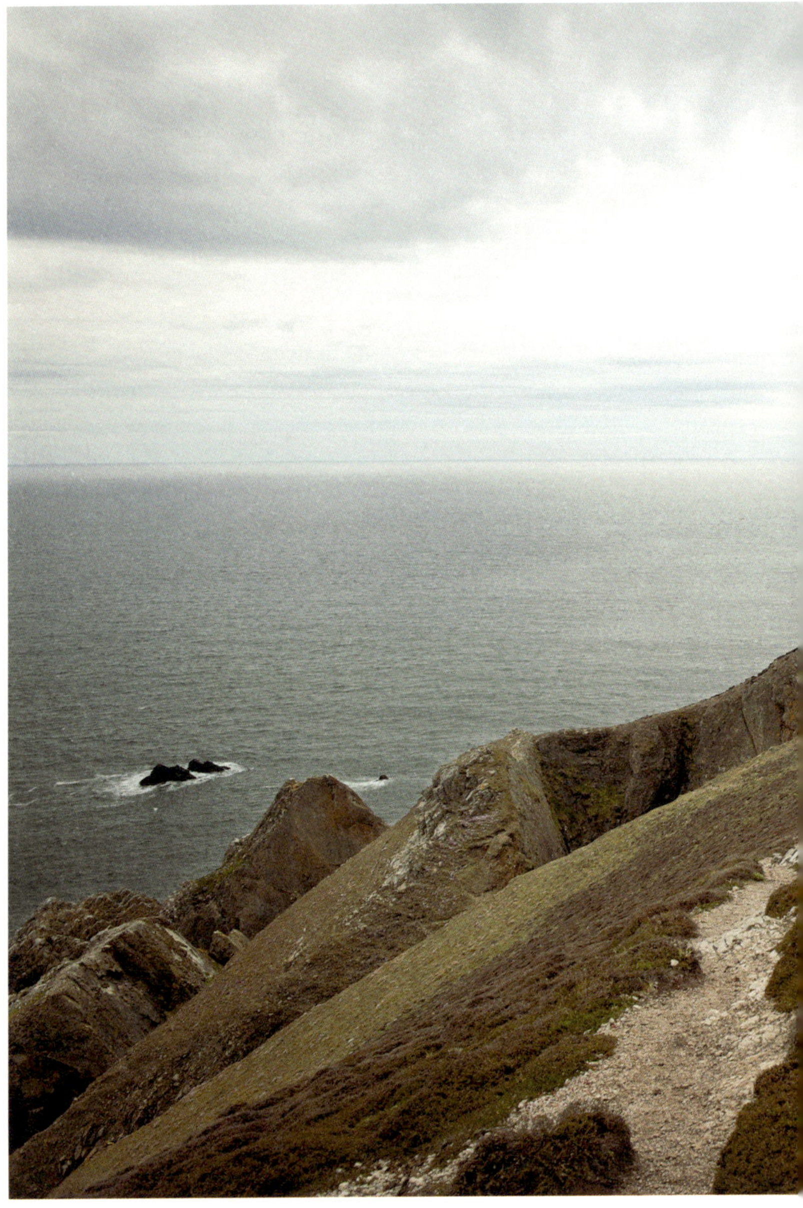

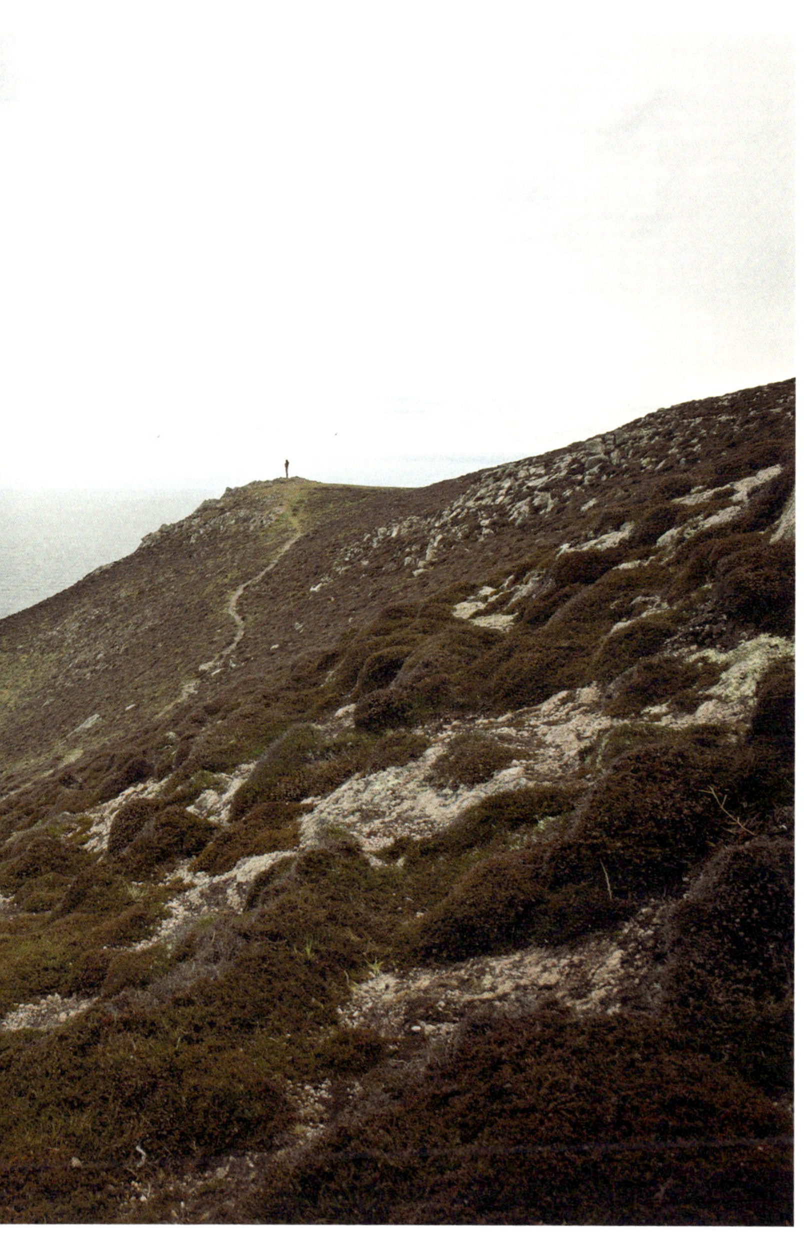

Lundy Island is a series of enclosures.

Often the island is invisible, enclosed in a steam-like fog stoked by Atlantic rain that drives the sheep against the westerly walls, their granite defence against the weather.

The sheep and the mist are the same shade of peat-soaked white.

Here and there on the rough road a strayed sheep stands like a desolate milestone pointing to a place I will never reach.

My cottage is itself an enclosure protecting me from the bandit weather. There's a stone wall round its boundary, then a double-door entrance that foils the wind. Then there's me, an enclosure of clothes and skin, and skull, and psychological shields, and ways of warding off the eyes of others, and Wizard of Oz-like illusions to hide behind.

But if the island is a series of enclosures — the pub, the shop, the huddle of buildings back-facing the prevailing wind, the belts of rhododendrons, the sheltered valley where Millcombe House sits, the low-scooped pools of fresh water, the abandoned granite quarries, the dug outs and drop downs, silent and deserted natural chambers, then, also…

The island is a grand exposure.

Rising up. Visible. Reared out of the Bristol Channel, where the Atlantic starts, an ocean of brave new worlds. This island is all edges, sometimes sharp, sometimes blurred, only 3 miles long by half a mile wide. Precipitous drops. Wherever you stand you are near to jumping off. This place is a flat earth theory of its own.

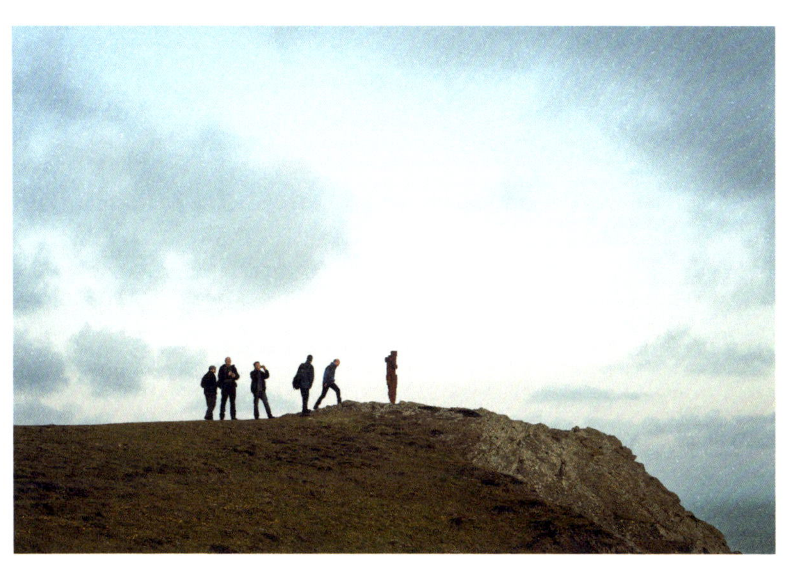

And over there, within easy sight of the old lighthouse, she's standing. The one who waits, as women have waited through history and time; for birth, for change, for news, for homecoming, for a boat visible on the horizon. Faith, patience, the long view.

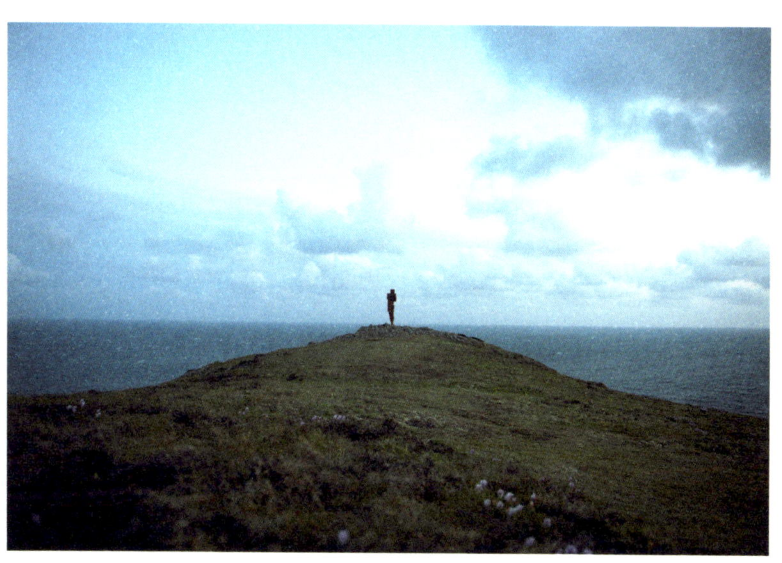

She isn't tall, this one — about my height — but she's strong. Slim ankles, nice breasts, proud like the prow of a ship, and they were always women too, those painted bodies cresting the waves.

The weather doesn't matter to this one in her iron oxide coat. Rust enclosed, body exposed. All defences are temporary.

What does she see, the light in riots round her head?

What does she see, positioned as a magnet for the stars?

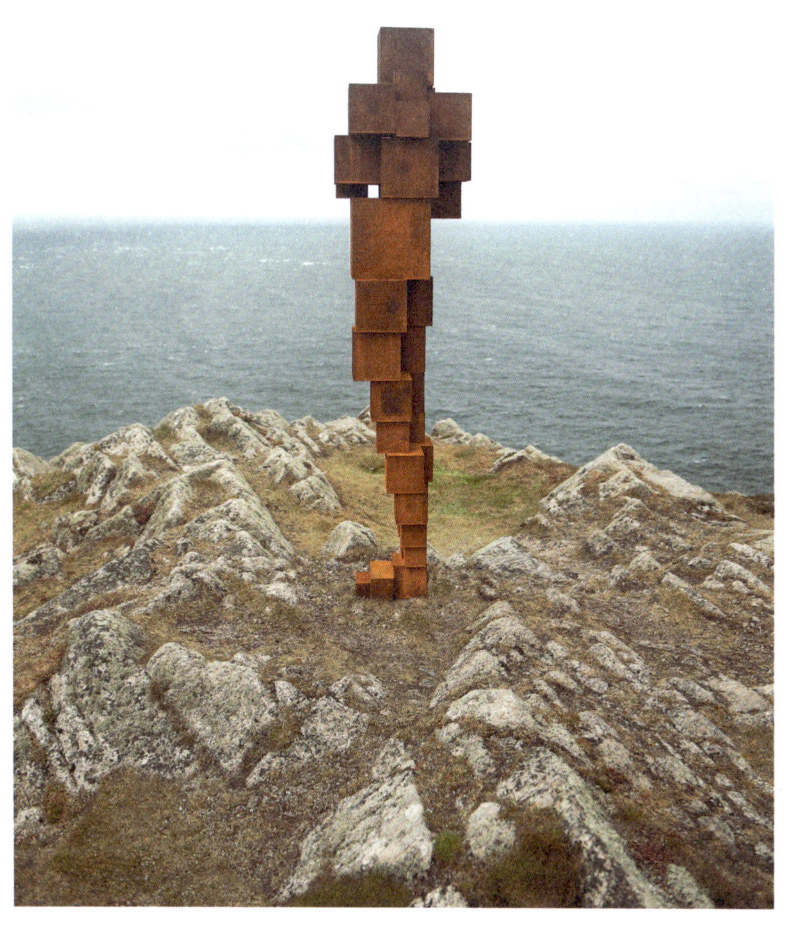

She's a totem. She's an anchorite. She's an anchor. She's a landing. She's the door at the rim of time. She's a widow. She's free. She's a memento mori. She's the beginning of your journey. She's what birds know. She's the Madonna of the Rocks. She's naked as a goddess. She's a lighthouse of the mind.

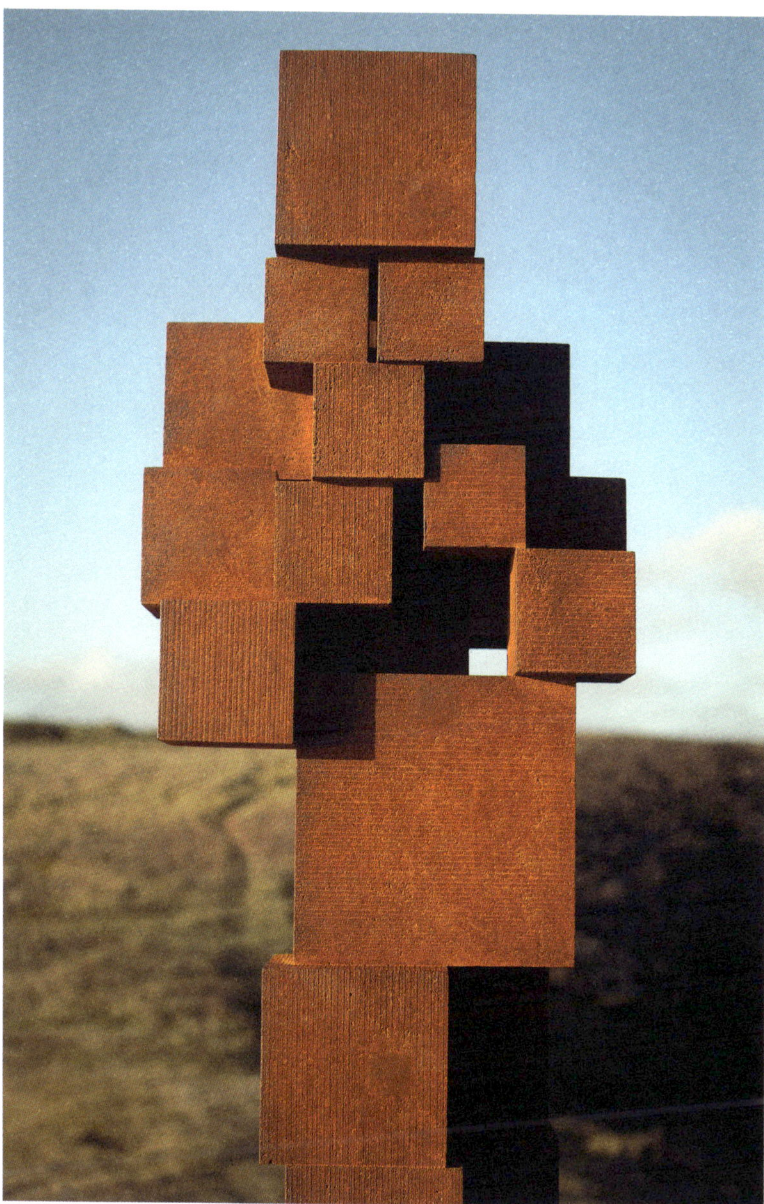

Of all the bodies in their places this is the one I would like to remain. She's like Ariel in The Tempest – the island's residing spirit, shaped into form by her master Prospero, energy temporarily present as mass.

Antony Gormley likes mass. His sculpture is dimensional, substantial. It takes muscle to make it and low-loaders to shift it.

But the mass is the form. What it houses is energy.

Art looks like an object but it isn't one; it's a process, a happening, an event, an experience, an explosion, a still small voice, a sound heard sometimes near, sometimes far off, a conversation, a work in progress. Many dreams. It's a relationship. It's a meeting. It is communication with the dead.

It is alive.

The energy caught inside the bodies will release in any number of ways. Wherever the bodies go next they will take with them an imprint of their first home – Saddell, or Lundy or the quiet bank of a canal. They come with a story.

And a record like this one will inspire other artists, other organisations, other donors to experiment with place and space. Public sculpture matters. Many people will never go to a gallery. Everybody goes outside. What we see in our daily round affects us. A significant object remedies banality.

It's all about us. All of us. The site where each of the bodies stand is us.

That's why anyone can own any art object. The moment you recognise it, really recognise it, both its significance and its significance to you – its image hangs in the gallery or remains on the street, but it locates inside you.

Temporary imprints in a temporary place.

That's how it is to be human. But our creative energy outlasts us, remakes itself in a new generation, a new spirit. We look at the objects we love – the boundless beautiful things that cross time. We're right to love them. We're right to make them. This is our way of describing who we are. But if everything were gone tomorrow, every museum, gallery, private collection, public monument, what would we do?

Grieve. Mourn. Begin again.

Mass is temporary. Energy is permanent.

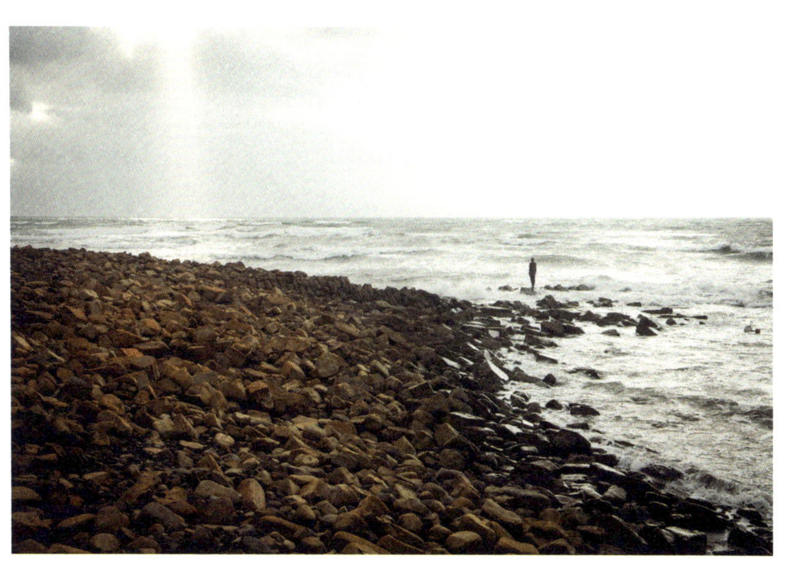

ACKNOWLEDGEMENTS

Making LAND a reality involved many helping hands. Antony Gormley wishes to thank:

The Landmark Trust: Alastair Dick-Cleland, Kasia Howard, Anna Keay, Vanessa Shaw, Caroline Stanford; Fiona Axford and Karen Chambers-Bellis (Clavell Tower, Kimmeridge); Mary Fisher (Lengthsman's Cottage); Hayley Trueman (Martello Tower); Glyn Baxter, Marilyn Donohue, Cy Neil, Sally-Ann Nixon and Joanne Quinby

Antony Gormley Studio: Philip Boot, Emily Constantinidi, Tamara Doncon, Giles Drayton, Ondine Gillies, Ashley Hipkin, Rosalind Horne, Alys Jenkins, Pierre Jusselme, Bryony McLennan, Alice O'Reilly; Michael Antrobus, Charlotte Booth and Maeve Butler

Sponsors: The LAND installation was funded by three very generous supporters of the Landmark Trust who prefer to remain anonymous, and with additional support from White Cube and the Canal & River Trust at Lowsonford

Momart: Iain Edwards, John Kidd, Guy Morey, Neville Redvers-Mutton, Stuart Wrenn and all Transport/Technical team members

The Morton Partnership: Ed Morton

Lundy: Jack Bater and the crew of M.S.Oldenburg; Derek Green, Lyndsey Green, Mike Jones and Beccy MacDonald; Jeremy Barker at Natural England; Kate Little at Torridge District Council

Lengthsman's Cottage: Tim Eastop, Ian Lane, Jon Pritchett and
Elizabeth Thomson at the Canal & River Trust; Dave Hunt
and Lesley Fahy at DHS Contractors Ltd

Kimmeridge Bay: Dan Barton, Robin Dukes and Adrian Ivory
at Owlsworth IJP Ltd; Anthony Bird, Alan Davies and John
Hartigan at Purbeck District Council; Piers Chichester, Rick
Hesslewood and Philip Mansel at the Smedmore Estate;
Peter Bellamy at Terrain Archaeology; Peter Christian at
Charter Build; Keith Miller and Charlotte Long-Clarke
at Historic England; Craig Loughlin at Marine Management
Office; Matthew Low at Natural England; Nick Shilton at
Shilton Cast Iron & Welding; Vertical Technology

Saddell Bay: David McCheyne; Tim Williams and Angus J
Gilmour at Argyll & Bute Council

Martello Tower: Julian Alexander at WMC Reade; Will Fletcher
at Historic England; Matt Harrowven at SCS UK Ltd;
David Saunders at Wavetrade Ltd

Communications: Marcus Stanton

Photography and Filming: Peter Cook; John Evetts; Nigel Dalby;
Lynn Harris; Tim Jones; Jon Lowe; John Miller and Jill Tate

Fabrication: Hargreaves Foundry; Davison Tyne Metal Ltd

Insurance: James Ferrer at Blackwall Green

Publication: John Morgan studio for design; Clare Richardson
for photography and Jeanette Winterson for her text

First published in 2016 by the Landmark Trust,
Shottesbrooke, Maidenhead, Berkshire, SL6 3SW
www.landmarktrust.org.uk

Artworks © 2016 Antony Gormley
Text © 2016 Jeanette Winterson
Photographs © 2016 Clare Richardson

Edited by Rosalind Horne
Designed by John Morgan studio
Printed by Musumeci S.P.A., Italy

Distributed by Thames & Hudson Ltd,
181A High Holborn, London, WC1V 7QX
www.thamesandhudson.com

ISBN 978 1 5262 0185 0

All Rights Reserved. No part of this publication may be
reproduced or transmitted in any form or by any means,
electronic or mechanical, including photocopy, recording
or any other information storage and retrieval system,
without prior permission in writing from the publisher.

British Library Cataloguing-in-Publication Data. A catalogue
record for this book is available from the British Library.

Sculptures by Antony Gormley: *Grip*, 2014 (illus. pp. 7, 29, 31,
33, 35 and 38–39); *Check*, 2014 (illus. pp. 13, 45, 48–49, 51, 53, 54
and 57); *Daze IV*, 2014 (illus. pp. 21, 96–97, 101, 103, 105 and 107);
Heed, 2014 (illus. pp. 61, 65, 68–69, 71, 73 and 115); *Stay*, 2014
(illus. pp. 79, 82–83, 85 and 87)

Antony Gormley LAND

A life-size cast iron sculpture was installed at each of the following five Landmark Trust sites across the British Isles, from May 2015 to May 2016: Saddell Bay, Mull of Kintyre; South West Point, Lundy; Clavell Tower, Kimmeridge Bay; Martello Tower, Aldeburgh and Lengthsman's Cottage, Lowsonford.

Commissioned by the Landmark Trust to mark its 50th anniversary year.

Project co-ordination by Caroline Stanford at the Landmark Trust and Bryony McLennan at Antony Gormley Studio.

The Landmark Trust is a building preservation charity. It rescues important historic buildings and offers them to everyone as amazing places to stay.

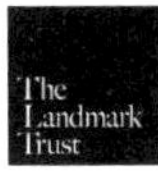

And there's you. The site where each of the bodies stands. Anyone can own a work of art. Just take it home with you.